4 DADA SUICIDES

4
DADA
Suicides

Selected texts of
ARTHUR CRAVAN, JACQUES
RIGAUT, JULIEN TORMA &
JACQUES VACHÉ

Introduced by Roger Conover,
Terry Hale & Paul Lenti, &
translated by Terry Hale, Paul
Lenti, Iain White &c.

Published by Atlas Press.
BCM ATLAS PRESS, LONDON WCIN 3XX
© 1995, Atlas Press
All English rights reserved
Rights to French texts as follows:
André Breton, La Confession dédaigneuse © 1924, Editions Gallimard; texts by Jacques
Rigaut © 1970, Editions Gallimard; texts by Arthur Cravan used with the permission of
Fabienne Lloyd Bénédict and Roger Lloyd Conover.
Printed in the UK by The Bath Press
A CIP record for this book is available from The British Library
ISBN 0 947757 74 0

Our thanks to
The Arts Council of Great Britain
&
The French Ministry of Foreign Affairs
(Sous-Direction de la Politique du Livre)
for financial assistance with this book.

Preface . . . 7.

■ Towards the beginning of the first issue of *La Révolution surréaliste* published in December 1924 there appeared the following announcement:

■ **Preface by**
Terry Hale

INQUEST

You live, you die. What has free will got to do with it? It seems you kill yourself in the same way as you dream. This is no moral problem we are posing.

IS SUICIDE A SOLUTION?

The editors of the journal — Pierre Naville and Benjamin Péret — promised that answers received by the *Bureau de recherches surréalistes* at 15, rue de Grenelle would be published in the January issue.

If the editors of *La Révolution surréaliste* held out hopes of a degree of unanimity in the replies that were sent in (as was certainly the case when André Breton launched his famous investigation into sexuality a few years later), then the inquest into suicide may only be regarded as something of a failure. The responses ranged from the predictably prosaic to the enthused. Francis Jammes, for example, a minor Symbolist poet whose work frequently extolled a return to Catholicism, replied: "Only a wretch would ask such a question, and if some poor child were to kill him or her self, you would be the murderer. The only resource open to you, should you have the slightest conscience left, is to throw yourselves into a confessional."

The majority of the answers, especially those sent in by the general public, were hardly more sophisticated. There were, however, two which stood out from among those by members of the Surrealist movement: René Crevel and Antonin Artaud. Crevel was an active member of the Surrealist movement from the moment of his heroic early involvement in the period of trances and "sleeping fits" until his death in 1935. In his first published work in book form (*Détours*, 1924) he wrote the following short Surrealistic spoof of a typical newspaper story concerning suicide: "Rue de Mauberge, a businessman threw himself from the ground-floor without causing himself any injury. Before a crowd could gather in the street, which is extremely busy, he went up to the sixth floor of his apartment building and suddenly crashed to the ground."

Crevel's reply to the investigation by *La Révolution surréaliste* is more thoughtful: "A solution? Yes. [...] It is said that one commits suicide from love, fear or venereal disease. Not so. Everyone is in love, or thinks they are. Suicide is a matter of conscious choice. Those who commit suicide are the ones who are not imbued with the quasi-universal cowardice of fighting against a certain feeling in the soul which is of such intensity that it has to be taken, until it is proved otherwise, for the truth. This is the only sensation that allows a person to embrace a solution that is clearly the fairest and most definitive solution of all, suicide. There is no love or hate which is simply fair or definitive. But the respect — in spite of myself and notwithstanding a tyrannical moral and religious upbringing — which I am bound to show to anyone who does not timorously withhold or restrain that impulse, that mortal impulse, leads me to envy more and more each day those persons whose anguish is so intense that they can no longer accept life's little games." Crevel, who was a Communist, killed himself on the eve of the Congress for the Defence of Culture organised in Paris, apparently disillusioned by his failure to bring about a rapprochement between Breton and the Soviet delegation.

For Artaud, suicide was less a solution than a hypothesis. "I claim the right to remain sceptical about suicide" — he wrote — "just as I am sceptical about all the rest of reality." Artaud goes on to claim that he finds the idea of suicide as a state of being incomprehensible: "I have no idea what things really are, no idea of any human state, nothing in the world works for me, nothing works in me. Life causes me atrocious suffering. I fail to reach any existing state." In place of the original question, he poses one of his own: "And almost certainly I died long ago, my suicide has already occurred. That is to say, I have *already been suicided*. But what would you think of an anterior state of suicide, a suicide which makes us retrace our steps, but on the other side of existence and not on the side of death?" Artaud did not in fact take his own life, but shortly before his death from cancer and after years of incarceration in a mental institution, he wrote his great text *Van Gogh: The Man Suicided by Society* (1947). This essay described his own situation as much as Van Gogh's, and is equally applicable to several of the writers in this collection: Cravan, Torma & perhaps Vaché.

In January 1925, another avant-garde review, *Le Disque vert* (edited by Franz Hellens and Henri Michaux), also published a series of articles on the question of suicide. As was the case with *La Révolution surréaliste*, the contributions by Crevel and Artaud were amongst the more intelligent, though it is curious to note that both authors make a number of significantly different points: "Is not the fear of suicide the best remedy against suicide?" (Crevel) "But even to get to the state of suicide, I must await my return to consciousness, I must have a free hand in all the articulations of my being. God has placed me in despair as if in a constellation of deadends whose radiance culminates in me. I can neither live nor die, nor can I not desire to die or live. And all mankind resembles me." (Artaud)

If the question of suicide was one of the dominant themes running through the literary and artistic life of France in the twenties and thirties, that was in part because Surrealism itself was ushered in by two suicides. Jacques Vaché was found dead in Nantes on 6 January 1919, apparently of an opium overdose and, just over a year later, Arthur Cravan disappeared in the Gulf of Mexico in a small rowing-boat, presumed drowned or eaten by sharks (though Roger Conover hints at a rather different outcome in his introduction here). These two deaths were followed in 1929 by the suicide of Jacques Rigaut and, four years later, by the disappearance in mysterious circumstances of Julien Torma on an Austrian hillside.

Vaché, Cravan, Rigaut and Torma have all been associated (somewhat loosely in the case of the latter) with Parisian Dada. All played a significant role in the formation of the French avant-garde. It was Jacques Vaché who introduced André Breton to the concept of 'Umour (which has precious little to do with the word it so closely resembles) while, more than seventy years after his supposed death, Arthur Cravan remains one of the most elusive yet intriguing figures in the annals of Dada. Despite his total unconcern for the good opinion of posterity, Jacques Rigaut's literary reputation has continued to grow steadily during the years since his death as new manuscripts have emerged. Finally, Julien Torma — the most nihilistic of Dadas — has left his inimitable imprint on the geography of that country where, in the words of Roger Shattuck, "a true stoicism meets a profound epicureanism": 'pataphysics.

Is suicide a solution? For Rigaut suicide was not so much a solution as a vocation. Concerning Vaché doubts have been raised as to how intentional his death was (Michel Leiris, for example, believed it was

an accident that was later disguised as self-destruction in order to lend
the event a literary quality). In the case of Cravan, suicide may have
been a solution (though not necessarily in the most obvious sense). As
for Julien Torma, it is very much to be doubted whether he believed in
solutions at all, at least in the accepted sense.

The writings of the four "authors" represented in this compilation
are thus, to some extent, simply a by-product of their extraordinary
lives: and a by-product that in each case was singularly undervalued by
its creator. For this reason the texts translated here have been prefaced
by a short biographical introduction, and followed by an account of
each author written by a contemporary (these sections have been given
the title of "witness," for want of a better word, and also because it is
precisely the lack of witnesses that has given these suicides such a rich
after-life).

The publishers would like to dedicate this book to the memory of
Paul Lenti as an expression of our thanks to him for his enthusiastic
involvement with this project.

■ ARTHUR CRAVAN

WANTED

ARTHUR CRAVAN 1887 – ?

STILL AT-LARGE: Fabian Avenarius Lloyd. A.K.A: Arthur Cravan. LAST SEEN: Salina Cruz, Mexico, 1918.

CONSIDERED EXTREMELY INTELLIGENT & DANGEROUS

Weight: 230 pounds. **Height:** 6 feet, 1 inch. **Distinguishing Physical Characteristics:** glass eye, broken nose. **Distinguishing mannerisms:** French accent. **Motto:** *"On ne me fait pas marcher moi."* **Languages:** French, English, German. **Suspected and Known Aliases:** Edouard Archinard, Isaac Cravan, Dorian Hope, Sebastian Hope, B. Holland, Robert Miradique, Marie Lowitska, W. Cooper, James M. Hayes. **Known Occupations:** Poet, professor, boxer, dandy, *flâneur*, forger, critic, sailor, prospector, card sharper, lumberjack, *bricoleur*, thief, editor, chauffeur.

■ 1. Q. Is Arthur Cravan still alive? And if he is living, then in what astonishing getup, behind what unimaginable disguise?

A. There are three figures, a man, a woman and someone else, each named Arthur Cravan. They are, in no particular order, a missing poet, an itinerant boxer and an elusive forger. They have carried on a century-long *ménage-à-trois*. Although each maintains a distinct *vita*, there is often identity slippage between them. Their characters sometimes merge into a metaphysical phenomenon that has no biographical counterpart.

■ 2. Whether Arthur Cravan vanished into thin air, drowned in high seas or reinvented himself on land sometime after he was last officially seen in November 1918, we may never know. There was no witness, no corpse, no note. What at first seems like one of the cleanest getaways in all of literature is in fact one of the most perplexing escapes in twentieth-century art, for his ambiguous exit was preceded by a life of invented personae, double identities and successful disguises, some of which are still unfolding more than seventy years after he was last spied on the Mexican coast preparing to sail for Buenos Aires to meet his wife.[1]

He had disappeared before, and had spoken to friends of doing so again. It was assumed that he would eventually resurface, bearing the passport of another country, camouflaged by the overcoat of a new

■ **Introduction: *Arthur Cravan* by Roger Lloyd Conover**

☐ Left: Arthur Cravan in boxing pose, ca. 1914. *Private coll.* Right: Cravan/Johnson fight poster, 1916. *Coll. Fabienne Bénédict.*

profession, or speaking the language of a new girlfriend. He was a world tramp; he knew that if he carried the circus within him, no cage or trainer could tame him. And so he did. He was a tireless traverser of borders and resister of orders — a mongrel of nations with a vexatious urge to disarm. He took experience in the most extreme doses and sought life in the most extreme conditions he could find. "I have twenty countries in my memory and I drag the colours of a hundred cities in my soul."[2] But his soul left no footprints. Only false scents. Dead ends.

For a long time, those close to him assumed that he would one day step back into view. He would choose some inappropriate moment to make his entrance, but all would be forgiven if the vagabond sailor or errant prince could prove he was Arthur Cravan — the Defiant, the Unpredictable, the Immoderate Arthur Cravan. The biceps of the boxer who left measured nineteen inches around. The halo of the poet who never returned encircled the spirit of Dada. One day a *fripier*, the next an elegant host in impeccable clothes, he safeguarded his inner truth with lies. He sought confrontation; he refused to bear arms. In defiance of war, he assumed the disguise of a soldier and hitchhiked to neutral ground. In defiance of punishment, he went out of his way to make enemies.

Some friends remained convinced for years that he was shadowing them; others felt haunted by his presence decades after they had last seen him. Over the years, many theories about his possible "survival" and "afterlife" have been posited.[3] Most of the speculation falls apart under scrutiny. But one theory has only grown in complexity, and concerns an unsolved mystery that is too Cravanesque to ignore. Unrecorded by historians of Dada, and little more than a footnote among students of forgery and Wildeana, it has nevertheless caused one writer to include Cravan "among the immortals in the ranks of forgers — that sparsely-populated group, containing only Major Byron, Ireland, Collier and a few others."[4] For more than seventy years, circumstantial evidence — with more than a few facts wedged between the cracks — has implicated Cravan as the alleged forger and vendor of apocryphal manuscripts by Oscar Wilde which caused a stir among Wilde scholars in the 1920s. The mysterious forger, signing his letters sometimes as "Monsieur André Gide" and sometimes as "Dorian Hope," Gide's secretary, was living in Paris and actively offering counterfeit material to book dealers and collectors in Dublin and London in 1921 and 1922.

This impostor's forgeries were so well-executed that their authenticity was initially vouchsafed by several Wilde experts, including Wilde's bibliographer and editor, Christopher S. Millard (pseudonym of Stuart Mason), whose reputation as a Wilde expert was then at its peak but suffered when he admitted his mistake. Robert Sherard (Wilde's first biographer), Vyvyan Holland (Wilde's son), C. Frederic Harrison (head of Brentano's, Paris) and other specialists were eventually brought into the case.

Meanwhile, a "Sebastian Hope," also writing from Paris, was offering similar material to Maggs Bros. (London), passing himself off as the representative of one of Wilde's former translators, Pierre Louÿs. In 1922, Mr. Figgis travelled to Paris to meet the "real" André Gide, who was vexed to learn of the bogus manuscripts being offered in his name. Without revealing his suspicions, Figgis set up a meeting with the pseudo-Gide, "Dorian Hope," who appeared "dressed like a Russian count with a magnificent fur-lined overcoat." Figgis became "convinced that he was the prime mover in the whole business." Gide wanted to press charges against Hope — he too suspected Cravan — but Figgis wouldn't join in the suit. Dorian Hope was never apprehended. The case remains open.

Dudley Edwards, who has provided the most detailed account of this deception, later wrote to all of the principals involved. "There is little doubt ... in the minds of any of the surviving participants ... that the cause of all the trouble was Dorian Hope, alias Sebastian Hope, alias André Gide, alias B. Holland, alias Fabian Lloyd (Arthur Cravan)...," he concluded. From the letters of Figgis, Millard, Vyvyan Holland, and Robert Sherard, Mr. Edwards wrote, "a picture can be built up." "It was he who, as Arthur Cravan, traded on pretending he was the son of Oscar Wilde and who ran the magazine *Maintenant* in which one of his

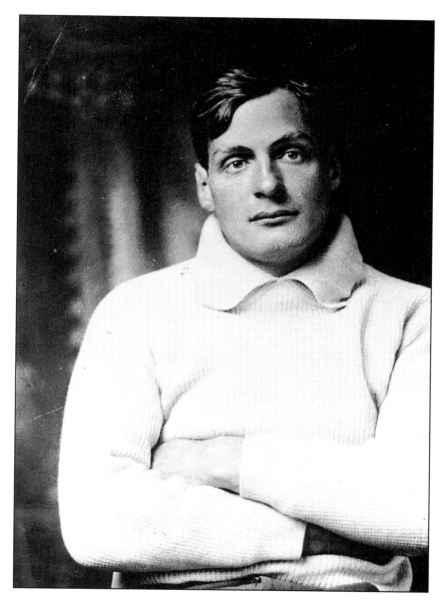

□ Arthur Cravan,
Barcelona, 1916.
Private coll.

stunts was a story that Wilde called on him in Paris on 23rd March 1913, and had a drink with him." (Wilde died in 1900). More than thirty years later, Vyvyan Holland and William Figgis were still perplexed by the unsolved forgeries. Holland wrote to Figgis on 23 September 1955:

I am interested in what you say about Dorian Hope... I always understood that he was my first cousin Fabian Lloyd. The Dorian came from Dorian Gray and the Hope from Adrian Hope who was one of the family trustees. He also called himself Arthur Cravan and edited a short-lived Dadaist magazine...

Millard's last reference to Cravan was also addressed to Figgis (7 May 1923). Suddenly a new alias surfaces, one that Cravan's father had already borrowed from his ancestry and assigned to his nephews to mask them from their father's (Oscar Wilde's) shame.[5] "Under the name B. Holland (Cravan) obtained many valuable books and letters from London and provincial booksellers and then disappeared and has not been heard of since."[6] If Holland was not Cravan's alias, then how uncanny the coded reference.

In 1957, many years after the last reported activities of the putative forger known as "Dorian Hope," a retired Philadelphia minister and bibliophile named Herbert Boyce Satcher came across Dudley Edwards' account and was startled to see the name "Dorian Hope." He remembered that this was the name used by "a strange sort of vagrant poet" whom he had known in New York in 1919 and 1920, whose refined verses were "completely at variance with his character..." He was using the name James M. Hayes, Satcher recalled, but as he passed through the gates to the train after their first meeting, "he slipped into my hand a visiting card on which the name 'Mr. Dorian

Hope' was engraved. He said I should use the name in any further communication with him . . . His appearance, as I remember it, was . . . rather derelict, with a velour hat down close to his eyes."[7]

Satcher recalled that it was a clergyman friend who had urged him to meet Hope/Hayes. The poet was described by his friend as the highest form of genius, but "a frank criminal." To know him, to meet him, his friend said, "is like knowing Poe or Maupassant or Verlaine or Musset or Whitman or Swinburne."[8] Satcher found eight letters that he had received from "Dorian Hope" during their brief acquaintance, all written on hotel stationery, all dated 1919-1920. One letter was signed "Eva, Dowager Empress of Iceland"; another, "Queen Mary." A final postcard dated 6 July 1920, bore a picture of a Cunard liner and was mailed from Southampton, England, eight months before "Gide/Hope" sent his first letter to Mr. Figgis from France. Satcher never heard from "Dorian Hope" again, but allows that "the correspondence certainly reveals him as an obvious homosexual." He finds it ironic, reading Dudley Edwards' account, that Fabian Lloyd should be "the 'Dorian Hope' of this strange tale":

The brother-in-law (Otho Lloyd) who was so shocked at Oscar Wilde's behaviour that he could not endure the prospect of his nephews even bearing the name of their father, could not have foreseen... that his own son (Fabian Lloyd) would turn out to be what he had so militantly condemned in Wilde, and with the added stigma of forgery, and the attempt to capitalise on Wilde's genius twenty years after his death.[9]

None of this proves that Cravan is Dorian Hope. Forensic handwriting analysis would help. But if the suspicions of Messrs. Figgis, Dudley, Holland, Millard, Edwards, Gide, Harrison and others are true, then Cravan was still in circulation well into the 1920s.

Quickly: Cravan disappears in Mexico in 1918; three years later Dorian Hope turns up in New York, then he is spotted in Paris, Amsterdam, and London. Whoever Dorian Hope was, he was unquestionably preoccupied with Oscar Wilde. Beyond that, he was someone strangely aware of Arthur Cravan; if not Cravan himself, then someone intent on incriminating Arthur Cravan. Someone who understood that Cravan made the perfect suspect and provided the perfect foil by virtue of his prior reputation and his missing person status. To wit: an impostor impersonating an impostor. Even if Cravan's handwriting was not involved in this hoax, it had all the flourishes of his signature.

A last witness to connect the final dots: in 1959, Guillot de Saix, the celebrated Wilde missioner in France, said he had met the *"faussaire Arthur Cravan"* in Paris in the 1930s, and that Cravan "had continued to make a living forging Wilde manuscripts for Charles Carrington, the shady publisher and purveyor of erotica in the rue de Châteaudun."[10] Carrington is also mentioned as one of Dorian Hope's contacts in Dudley Edwards' account.

Putting aside the question of Cravan's survival, these stories add an almost unbelievably rich field of speculation on which to plot the known and unknown, imagined and unimagined, literary and sexual transpositions and tensions of Gide: Cravan, Wilde: Cravan and Gide: Wilde. Gide and Wilde were once close, but wrote equivocally and grew wary of one another over time. Cravan achieved notoriety for his irreverent portrait of Gide which appeared in *Maintenant* at a time when Gide, because of the anarchistic character Lafcadio, was virtually worshipped by the young writers of the day. But unknown to the public then, and still generally unacknowledged today, is the fact that Gide had modelled the amoralist and conman in *Les Caves du Vatican*

(1914) after Cravan. Cravan was simply acting in character when he took corrective, insulting measure of Gide.[11] Finally, Cravan was psychically possessed by his uncle Oscar, even to the point of imitating his dandiacal manner of dress and claiming to be his son. Thirteen years after Wilde's death, he ran an exclusive, seemingly ingenuous "interview" with his uncle in *Maintenant* (*Oscar Wilde est Vivant!*) causing newspapers in New York to assign correspondents in Paris to investigate the story.[12]

■ **3.** For Cravan, suicide was an act. He once drew a full house to the *Noctambules* in Paris by advertising his sincere intention to end his life before a paying public; he would replace the traditional carafe of water with a bottle of absinthe; "for the benefit of the ladies," he would wear only a jockstrap and deliver his pre-suicide *récit* with his balls draped on the table. Suicide was a means of, not an end to, performance. Threatening to take his life, then chastising his audience for making a social event of death, was a signature Cravan technique.

He had a natural gift for transgressive, offensive behaviour — the other side of which was sympathy and charisma — a fluid spell he could as easily cast on a crowd of spectators as on a policeman whose distrust he registered. He was most content if he went too far, if he incited such outrage that his fluidity was called upon. Mina Loy called his provocations "pantomimic atrocities on the spectator's habitual expectations." She explained his assaults as his way of taking revenge on a world that has always exploited the artist, as defences against a world that demolishes its superiors. "He worked to maintain his reality by presenting an unreality of himself to the world — to occupy itself with — while he made his spiritual getaway."[13]

His most polemical text is probably his review of *L'Exposition des Indépendants* in Paris in 1914. His vilification of the exhibiting artists was so severe that he was incarcerated and brought before a tribunal of peers. His most renowned "lecture" was at the New York Independents Exhibition in 1917; on this occasion he threw his dirty laundry at the audience and actually began to undress before being manacled and hauled off to jail. This performance has long been

☐ Cravan at an outdoor training session, Barcelona, 1916.

recognised as one of the crowning achievements of pre-Dada in New York. His code of combat was adjusted for non-artistic venues. When WWI broke out in 1914, he was a Swiss "subject" living in France. Determined not to serve in the armed services of any country, but to choose his own allies and enemies instead, he slid successfully past border patrols into Spain, where in 1916 he engaged in the famous boxing match with former World Heavyweight Champion Jack Johnson. Cravan is surely the only boxer in the history of the sport to have praised Jack Johnson and Oscar Wilde as twin heroes. The three form an odd triumvirate. All were notorious non-conformists, all had schooled themselves in classics, and all were forced into exile for their habits. The Johnson/Cravan face-off was as much a collaboration as a contest; both knew they could draw a crowd. Johnson needed a fight, and Cravan needed a percentage of the gate in order to make his next port of call, New York.

By this time, Cravan had already retired his natural name and his natural identity, Fabian Lloyd, in favour of a para-self, an *alter idem*, a new biographical reality. The person who existed as Fabian Avenarius Lloyd from 1887 to about 1912 became a person of precarious biographical status thereafter. This was not simply a change of driver's licence, but a repersonification. If there was a suicide, it was not tropical, but tropological; and it was not Arthur Cravan's, but Fabian Lloyd's.

■ **4.** For the last decade of his known life, the period during which he was occasionally writing and boxing, Cravan expressed — in person and on the page — an obsession with his own body. He was interested in its history. He built its reputation. At the same time, he existentialised its future; he imagined self-erasure. He wanted his life

□ Spanish newspaper caricature of Cravan and wife at the time of the Johnson fight.

to be both virtual and actual, to exist in conceptual as well as biological space. This required more than a fusing of life and art; it required tormenting and pleasuring his life *as* art. His abject lines expressed these ambitions, as did his passionate embrace of contradictions:

> You must dream your life with great care
> Instead of living it as merely an amusement
> (*Des Paroles / Some Words*)

When he stepped into the ring, he invariably announced himself as the "Poet and Boxer Arthur Cravan," as if dividing himself in two. This was usually followed by a long string of other pedigrees (hotel thief, snake-charmer, grandson of the Queen's Chancellor, nephew of Oscar Wilde, poet with the shortest haircut in the world...) which must have seemed equally incongruous to ringside observers. But "poet and boxer" touched the right note; those were his co-existent and extreme souls. In his masculine comportment was a feminine negotiation of opposites, a willing of reluctant inner brides. In the boxing ring, the figure thrusting and receiving was vulnerable and volatile, subtle and brute, respectful and taunting. In his stanzas, masculinity and femininity, anxiety and repose, eloquence and slang, sentiment and sexuality were likewise the diametric poles that generated a voltaic cell of poetic power. "What soul disputes my body?" he asks in *Hie*. The answer: "My fatal plurality!"

Genius is nothing more than an extraordinary manifestation of the body.
— ARTHUR CRAVAN

■ **5.** Dadaism is the movement usually associated with Cravan's name, but the movement he enjoyed most was physical. Dancing, fucking, boxing, walking, running, eating, swimming. He loved the taste and smell of the body's first issues — urine, shit, spit, sweat — and regarded these fundamental utterances as proto-texts. *"Je mangerais ma merde,"* he proudly proclaimed. His poems and essays were secondary aspirations — but in their gestural sweep and postural fix they can also be read as bodily manifestations, lines delivered or speech executed like ring exercises, by-products of a body always in motion — crossing borders, slicing sensibilities, murdering reputations, knocking heads. Cravan felt his muscular advantage even as he got off a good combination of nouns. In its intentional provocation, much of Cravan's editorial writing is the literary equivalent of bullying; the knock-out instinct dominated his critique.

As a *conférencier*, he would arrive at the *Société des Savantes* in tights, waving a pistol and firing shots into the air. He would praise athletes, homosexuals, prostitutes, thieves, madmen, etc. He would read his poems balancing first on one foot and then on the other, sometimes throwing his briefcase and other projectiles into the air along with verbal arrows he aimed at the audience. Long before the advent of performance art, his literary presentations were strenuous, even dangerous performances.

■ **6.** Even before he had reasons to be elusive, plotting Cravan's co-ordinates was a navigational challenge. His parents were English, his language was French, his passport was Swiss. His last-known driver's licence was issued in Berlin, his last-known address was Mexico City. As a teenager, he was expelled from boarding school and rode boxcars from New York to California, working as a butcher, orange-picker and lumberjack along the way. In his 20s, he studied the classics, boxed in Athens and Barcelona, and lectured on modern art in Paris and New York. It is impossible to understand the movement without somehow coming to grips with his role. As André Breton put it, Cravan's life is the single best barometer for measuring the impact of the avant-garde between 1912 and 1917.

With no foreknowledge of Dada, Cravan was the forefather of Dada. During these years, he established himself as the incontestable master of negative appeal; he paved the way for Tristan Tzara's anti-art slogans well before the opening of Cabaret Voltaire. Whether writing reviews that landed him in jail, or responding to invitations from Marcel Duchamp and Walter Conrad Arensberg that required bail, Cravan was a guaranteed box office and sidewalk success. "Glory is a scandal," he proclaimed. "Let me state once and for all: I do not wish to be civilised."

He made a lasting impression on his contemporaries, who never tired of describing his personality, appearance or behaviour. Blaise Cendrars, Marcel Duchamp, Francis Picabia, Kees van Dongen, Félix Fénéon, Ossip Zadkine, André Salmon, Gabrielle Buffet-Picabia, Georges de Solpray, Louis-de-Gonzague Frick, and Walter Conrad Arensberg were among his friends, co-conspirators and sympathisers. Mina Loy occupied a place in his life that none of these came close to.[14] Most of his enemies weren't visible to him, but André Gide, Robert Delaunay, Guillaume Apollinaire and Marie Laurencin are on record. They were threatened by his presence and didn't like his tactics, whether in the pages of *Maintenant* or in more direct

□ Fabian Lloyd/
Arthur Cravan as a
student, Lausanne,
ca. 1908. *Collection
Roger L. Conover.*

encounters.[15] *Maintenant* was a violently polemical journal, with no regard for fair play. During its brief existence, Cravan used it as his personal loudspeaker to attack those who didn't attack him, to advertise his friends' cafés, to bring down artists' reputations, to vent his wrath on the public, to publish his poems and to praise his unlikely heroes. Consisting entirely of Cravan's own writing, presented under many pseudonyms, its purpose was not to identify talent, but to insult it: "If I write, it is to infuriate my colleagues; to get myself talked about and to make a name for myself. A name helps you succeed with women and in business..."

Maintenant has come to be regarded as the most important forerunner of *391* and other pre-war Dada publications. Cravan simply saw it as a warm-up for public brawls and sparring sessions in the gymnasium.

■ **7.** Critical warning: this book presents Cravan with three writers who occupy a much cozier position with him here than they did in life. This is guilt by association. We can finally read Arthur Cravan. Must he be immediately woven into a larger pathological tradition of impostureship, narcissism, suicide, subversion, disappearance, deviance, protest, longing, hallucination, obsession and exclusion? Must we already link him to other examples of "his kind," the *sui generis*, the "special case," in order to give him a place?

It is tempting to do this: to consider his case in the context of other blurred lives, exceptional accidents and alter-artists like Arthur Rimbaud, B. Traven, Ret Marut, Hal Croves, Ambrose Bierce, William Herman Rulofson, Roland Barthes, Thomas Chatterton, Felix-Paul Greve, Stéphane Mallarmé, Jean Genet, Raymond Roussel,

Elsa von Freytag-Loringhoven, Georges Bataille, Alfred Jarry, Anna Tsvetaeva, Guy Debord, Jean-Jacques Lequeu, Francesco Colonna, François Villon, Gérard de Nerval, Paul Verlaine, Baron Corvo, Frederick William Rolfe, Dominique Aury, Pauline Réage, Comte de Lautréamont, Isidore Ducasse, Charles Lassailly, Jacques Rigaut, Jacques Vaché and Julien Torma. But this is to give him a home, to fix him a place, and to assimilate his identity into a curriculum. Is this to respect the freedom of this angel-criminal, or to trap him? Canon is the cage he escaped. That is why he is still at large.

Coming suddenly upon a spider spinning an absorbing web around the chrysalis of a butterfly this morning, I watched it.

■ **8.** Despite a mythologising necrophilia that has attached itself to Cravan on the part of everyone from the Surrealists to the Pataphysicians to the Situationists to the Sex Pistols, the chrestomathy which follows is the most extended instalment of his texts yet to appear in English. These texts, prologue to a larger collection in preparation, are among the relatively few literary traces that he left. Rather than thinking of them as part of his legacy (*lettre*), I propose thinking of them as by-products of a combustible compound which did not completely succeed in eliminating all traces of itself (*l'être*). If Arthur Cravan had totally fulfilled his quest, he would have taken this residue with him, and left only the imprint of his gestures on our imagination. He put all of his genius into his life; when life combusted, these remnants of talent were left.

□ Above: Photo-
graph from an
(inaccurate)
identity card, 1914.
Right: Cravan's
signature.

mon nom véritable est Fabian Lloyd. Arthur Cravan

■ Some two years ago, when kindly people still gullible enough to believe in dentists' adverts still had faith in ju-jitsu and French boxing, a handful of listless dandies strove to turn themselves into Englishmen.

By Hercules! How out of date that fashion has become, time has petrified it. Only those who come from backwoods such as the Latin Quarter still rig themselves up in knickerbockers and a cap.

Today, in contrast, everyone is American. It is essential to be American, or at least to look like you are one, which is exactly the same thing.

Everyone does. It is the only way to be fashionable.

Everyone does, I tell you, from the most miserable wretches to the most extravagant fops.

When I say everyone, you must understand I mean everyone who is slightly sporty and capable of being of interest to us. Because all the rest is just trash. To be American, it is understood, is to be an American of the United States, not a peanut from South America.

In America, you are an American only if you come from the United States, just as in France no one would reasonably think of themselves as French unless they came from Paris.

Back home, the first imitation of Americans began with the public admiration for the cakewalk dancers. I would allow that American track athletes were not without some influence. Finally, Wilbur Wright gave a strong impetus to the nascent fashion, because to be American was to have the stamp of genius. But with the advent of the Yankee boxers, Joe Jeannette and Willie Lewis among others,

■ **To Be or Not To Be . . . American**

everyone, to make use of a cliché, went berserk. Paris quite rightly idolised them.

Overnight, everyone began to chew gum, to spit and to swear as well as any American. Everyone floated around in clothes two sizes too large. The most gangly of youths had shoulders as broad as a tree. Everyone put on American shoes, wore American collars. Everyone shaved and sported a bowler hat at an angle.

There were a goodly number of advantages to be drawn from being American. First of all, America is one of the nations which best protects its subjects abroad. Next, Americans are feared since they know how to box — or at least are supposed to. Americans come from far away, which is by no means prejudicial. What's more, at a time when everyone needed to carry the label of a profession, barring outlaws, when one man is proud to be a joiner, another a Naturalist poet, others journalists, house-breakers, painters or long-distance runners, he, the American, is an American, and nothing else. By this right, every salon opens its doors to him. Recognising him for an American, no one would dream of wondering what he does for a living.

And if ever a more perspicacious gentleman enquires out of curiosity:

"But what does that gentleman do?"

"The gentleman is an American," will be the invariable reply.

The first gentleman will always feel that everything has been revealed to him.

To be an American, therefore, is to have a status.

To be American is the only thing of importance and everybody is one. Only those who are blind or stupid, or are deliberately lying, will disagree.

To be sure, everyone is American, but more or less convincingly. It is not difficult to pass for an American American however.

"More difficult than you might think," someone interposed. "You have to learn English or, more precisely, American."

"You couldn't be more mistaken! A true American never talks."

"You're pulling my leg."

"Not at all, sir. Americans speak in monosyllables, the most elementary acquaintance with their language is sufficient, and I propose that a simple yes (pronounced Yea), repeated once a minute, is sufficient to sustain a conversation. You will admit that even the most dull-witted can remember that."

On the other hand, it is obvious that the use of an oath, such as *hell*, for example, grunted at every turn, makes good copy, while to know the rudiments of the jig, the national dance of Americans, is tantamount to a masterpiece. In America, the execution of a little jig demonstrates intense satisfaction, and you may certainly make a few of the movements of this frisky dance if you suddenly feel happy, if you hear music, or even if the humour just takes you. You may dance it wherever you are, in a bar, in the street, without paying the slightest attention to the stuck up noses of the people about you. In addition, and for your guidance, here are some tips on how to become the most polite of American gentlemen:

Be a whisker taller than the norm.

Be clean-shaven.

Part your hair in the middle.

Chew.

Spit in the drawing-room.

Wipe your nose with your fingers.

Never speak.

Dance the jig.

Carry your money loose in your pocket, not in a wallet.

Always keep your hat on your head.

Greet people by raising your forefinger to the brim of your hat.

Always look busy.

Hang around bars drinking nothing but "American drinks."

Despise women.

With respect to your wardrobe, shoes and American collars are indispensable with flowing clothes. Those of your grandfather will suit you down to the ground if you are twenty years old. Bowlers and felt hats are very becoming.

Caps with outrageous peaks are tolerable only for boxers or those who wish to pass as such, which is exactly the same thing.

Always remember this wonderful maxim: I am Number One, my neighbour is Number Two.

And, above all else, crown yourself with arrogance. Cheek is everything. The time is not far off when a man who stops another man in the street and asks for a light will be called a cheapskate.

If you are dressed as an American, you can accost anyone in the street in this manner:

"I say! (which means: Hey!) Do you have a cigar?"

If you are given one, never proffer a word of thanks.

That is an American for you.

Of late, it has become extremely fashionable to pass oneself off as a Negro.

I would happily hold forth on this subject, but I fear to exhaust your patience . . . and myself.

■ Decks lulled by the rhythm of the Ocean,
While in the air gases swirl like twirling tops,
And the heroic express arrives whistling into Le Havre,
Athletic sailors approach like bears.
New York! New York! How I want to inhabit you!
There I see the marriage of science
And industry
With bold modernity,
And in the Palaces,
Globes
Which dazzle the retina
With their ultra-violet rays;
The American telephone
And the tranquillity
Of elevators . . .

The defiant ship of the English line
Welcomed me aboard with breathless expectation,
Well-content with the luxury, such as the electrical fittings
Which flood the vibrant cabin with light,
Of the beautiful turbine-driven ship.
The cabin ablaze with copper columns,
Upon which, by seconds, my drunken hands delight
Suddenly to tremble in the cool metal,
And quench my appetite in this vital plunge,

■ **Whistle**

As the sharp smell of fresh varnish
Clearly shrieked the date on which, leaving all bills behind,
I rolled about like an egg in the crazy greenness of the grass.
How my shirt intoxicated me! Just to feel its motion,
Not unlike that of a horse, at one with nature!
How I wanted to jig forwards! How I wanted to rush on!
And how good it was on the bridge, tossed about by the music;
And how powerful is the sensation of cold
When first one breathes!
At last, unable to whinny or to swim,
I acquainted myself with the passengers
Entranced by the continuous bobbing of the waterline;
And, until together we espied the morning tramways scurrying toward
the horizon,
And the facades of buildings quickly turning pale,
Under rain and under sun and under the dome of stars,
Without incident we sailed for seven times twenty-four hours!

Trade favoured my young initiative:
Eight million dollars earned from canned goods
And the well-known brand bearing Gladstone's head
Yielded ten steamers each of four thousand tons
Flying flags embroidered with my initials
And stamping my commercial power upon the waves.
I also own my first locomotive:
Puffing out steam like snorting horses,
Yet bending its will under expert hands,
It rushes by madly, rigid upon its eight wheels.
It pulls the long convoy on its adventurous trek,

Into green Canada, through virgin forests,
And across my bridges with their caravan or arches,
At daybreak, the familiar fields of wheat;
Or, imagining a town amidst starry night,
It whistles penetratingly through valleys,
Dreaming of the oasis: the station in the heaven of glass,
Amidst the thicket of rails it crosses by thousands,
Where, trailing its long white cloud, it rolls its thunder!

■ **André Gide** ■ As I was feverishly dreaming, after a long spell of the most dreadful idleness, of growing suddenly very rich (My God! How often do I dream of that!), as I was reflecting on my unfulfilled projects, and getting increasingly worked up at the thought of dishonestly, and wholly unexpectedly, rising to affluence by means of poetry — I have always tried to consider art as a means and not as an end — I said to myself cheerfully: "I ought to pay a call on André Gide. He's a millionaire. What a lark — I shall take the old *littérateur* for a ride!"

Almost immediately (how quickly one can warm to an idea!) I bestowed the gift of prodigious success on myself. I dropped Gide a line, mentioning my kinship with Oscar Wilde. Gide agreed to see me. I was like a dream to him given my size, my shoulders, my beauty, my eccentricities, my words. Gide was infatuated, he would do anything for me. We were already on our way to Algeria — he declined the journey to Biskra, though I fully intended to drag him as far as the Somali Coast. My face was soon tanned, because I have always been a little ashamed of being white. And Gide paid for the private compartments, the thoroughbred mounts, the palaces, and for our partners. In short, I made a reality of some of my thousands of souls. Gide paid, paid and paid again; and I even dared to hope that he would not sue me for damages when I admitted to him that following the unhealthy profligacy of my leaping imagination he had sold everything barring his trusty Normandy farm in order to satisfy all my modern child's caprices.

Ah! I can still see myself as I imagined myself then, my legs stretched out on the seat of the Mediterranean express, coming out with the most outlandish suggestions to entertain my Maecenas.

One could say of me that I have the morals of an Androgide. But will anyone say it?

In any event, my little projects of exploitation were so unsuccessful that I want to take my revenge. I should nonetheless add, so as not to unduly alarm provincial readers, that I took an overwhelming aversion to M. Gide the day when, as I said earlier, I realised that I would not get ten centimes out of him and that, what's more, this shabby tail-coat permits himself to wipe the floor, *for reasons of excellence*, with the naked cherub that goes by the name of Théophile Gautier.

In short, I went to pay a call on M. Gide. I seem to remember that at the time I did not possess a suit, something I regret to this day as it would have made it easy for me to have dazzled him. As I approached his house, I repeated to myself the brilliant remarks that I would try to slip into the course of our conversation. A moment later I rang the bell. A maid opened the door (M. Gide does not have any flunkies). I was shown to the first floor and I was asked to wait in a sort of tiny cell created by a right angle in the corridor. As we proceeded, I glanced with curiosity into all the different rooms, trying to get an idea in advance of the guest bedrooms. Then, I was sitting in my own little corner. The leaded glass windows, which looked like reproductions to me, allowed the daylight to fall across a writing-desk on which sheets freshly dampened with ink lay scattered. Naturally, I did not fail to commit the tiny indiscretion that you may imagine. And it is for that reason that I can inform you that M. Gide takes tremendous pains polishing his prose and that he will hand over to the type-setters hardly anything before the fourth draft.

The maid came back to show me downstairs. As I went into the drawing-room, a number of unruly pugs began barking. Not an auspicious start. All the same, I had plenty of time to look around. Some modern, and slightly unfetching, articles of furniture in a spacious room; blank walls (a suggestion of simplicity or a suggestion of simple-mindedness) and above all an attention to detail which was extremely Protestant in arrangement and cleanliness. I even broke out for a moment in a rather unpleasant sweat at the thought that I had perhaps soiled the carpet. I would probably have pushed my curiosity a bit further, or even ceded to the exquisite temptation to put some small object in my pocket, if I had been able to dismiss the very distinct impression that M. Gide was spying on me through some secret little hole in the wallpaper. If I am mistaken, I beg M. Gide to have the goodness to accept my immediate and public apologies for the harm I have occasioned his dignity.

Finally, the man himself appeared. (What struck me the most from this moment was that he offered me absolutely nothing except for a seat while on the stroke of four o'clock in the afternoon a cup of tea, if one is a martyr, or better still a little alcohol and Eastern tobacco is considered, quite rightly, in the best European society as creating the indispensable ambience for such a meeting to be memorable.)

"M. Gide," I began, "I have taken leave to call on you, though I feel myself duty bound to inform you straight off that I far prefer, for example, boxing to literature."

"Literature, however, is the only terrain on which we may profitably encounter one another," he replied rather dryly.

I thought: "He certainly lives life to the full."

We spoke about literature therefore, and as he asked me the following question which must be particularly dear to him: "Which of my works have you read?" I announced without moving a muscle,

"Your work makes me afraid to read it." I imagine that M. Gide must have visibly flinched at that. Then, one by one I managed to place those famous phrases, the ones I had been repeating to myself earlier, while imagining that the novelist would be grateful to be able to exploit the nephew as he had the uncle. First of all, I carelessly let fall: "The Bible is the greatest best-seller of all time." A moment later, as he showed sufficient consideration to ask after my parents: "My mother and I," I said drolly, "were not born to understand each other."

The subject of literature came up again, and I took advantage of the fact to abuse at least two hundred living writers, a number of Jewish writers, especially Charles-Henri Hirsch, and to add: "Heine is the Christ of modern Jewish writers." From time to time, I threw a discreet and malicious glance at my host, who repaid me with stifled laughter, but who, I ought to say, lagged a long way behind me, content, it would seem, just to listen as he had probably not prepared anything.

On one occasion, breaking off a philosophical discussion and composing my features to resemble a Buddha whose lips would unseal themselves once in every ten thousand years, I murmured: "The greatest Joke is to be found in the Absurd." When the time came for me to take my leave, I enquired in a very tired and elderly voice: "Monsieur Gide, how are we doing for time?" Discovering that it was a quarter-to-six, I rose to my feet, affectionately shook the artist's hand and left carrying in my head a portrait of one of our most notorious contemporaries, a portrait which I shall sketch here if my dear readers would be gracious enough to grant me a moment of their attention.

M. Gide resembles neither a love-child nor an elephant nor yet the average man. He looks like an artist; and the only compliment, disagreeable as it is, I shall pay him is that his tiny pluralism derives from the fact that he could easily be mistaken for a ham actor. There is nothing remarkable about his bone structure; his hands, which upon my word are very white, are those of an idler. Overall, his frame is very small. M. Gide must weigh about 55 kilos and measure around 1 metre 65 centimetres in height. His deportment betrays a prose-writer *who will never compose a single line of verse*. In addition, the artist has an unhealthy face, and tiny petals of skin larger than dandruff detach themselves from somewhere around his temples, an indisposition which people seek to explain away by saying vulgarly that someone "peels."

However, the artist entirely lacks the noble ravages of the spendthrift who squanders his fortune and his health. No, a hundred times no: on the contrary, the artist seems to give every indication that he looks after himself meticulously, that he is very hygienic, and that he is miles away from a Verlaine who supported his syphilis like a languor, and I believe, in the absence of any denial on his part, that I do not venture too far in affirming that he frequents neither prostitutes nor low dives; and it is on the basis of such clues that we are happy to report, as we have already had occasion to do, that M. Gide is a prudent man.

I only saw M. Gide once in the street. He was leaving my home. There was only a short distance to the corner of the street where he would disappear from sight and I saw him halt in front of the window of a bookshop, even though there was a shop selling surgical instruments and a confectioner's nearby . . . Since then, M. Gide has written to me once and I have never seen him again.

I have revealed the man, and I would willingly now reveal his work if, on a single point, I could do so without repeating myself.

■ What soul disputes my body?   ■ **Hie!**
I hear music:
Will I be swept away?
I so adore dancing
And other physical foolishness
I feel it is plain
That had I been a young girl
I would have been utterly corrupted.
But, since I've already plunged myself
Into this illustrated review,
I can swear that I have never seen
Such enchanting photographs:
The lazy ocean cradles the funnels,
I see in the port, on the decks of steamships,
Among the indiscriminate merchandise,
Sailors mixing with stokers;
Bodies polished like machines,
A thousand things from China,
Fashions and inventions;
Then, ready to cross town
In the tranquillity of automobiles,
Poets and boxers.
This evening, how great my disgust
That, despite so much sadness,
Everything seems beautiful?

Money which is real,
Peace, vast enterprises,
Buses and graves;
Fields, sports, mistresses,
Even the inimitable life of hotels.
I would like to be in Vienna and Calcutta,
Catch every train and every boat,
Lay every woman and gorge myself on every dish.
Man of fashion, chemist, whore, drunk, musician, labourer, painter,
acrobat, actor;
Old man, child, crook, hooligan, angel and rake; millionaire,
bourgeois, cactus, giraffe, or crow;
Coward, hero, Negro, monkey, Don Juan, pimp, lord, peasant, hunter,
industrialist,
Flora and fauna:
I am all things, all men and all animals!
What next?
Assume a distinguished air,
Manage to leave behind perhaps
My fatal plurality!
And while the moon,
Beyond the chestnut trees,
Harnesses her greyhounds,
And, as if in a kaleidoscope,
My abstractions
Elaborate variations
On my body's
Harmonies,
May my fingers,

Stuck to my delighted keys,
Imbibe fresh palpitations,
Beneath immortal movements
My braces thrill;
And, ideal pedestrian
Of the Palais-Royal,
I brazenly get drunk
Even on bad smells.
A complete mixture
Of elephant and angel;
Reader, under the moon I serenade
Your future misfortune,
Armed with so much logic,
That, lacking sensual desire,
I can anticipate the stench of rut,
Cunt, pipe, water, Africa and funereal repose,
Behind lowered blinds,
The calm of the brothel.
Some balm, O my reason!
Paris is atrocious and I hate my home.
Already the cafés stand darkened.
The only place left, O my neuroses!
Is the bright stabling
Of the urinals.
I can no longer remain outside.
Here is your bed; be stupid and go to sleep.
But, the last tenant of all,
Who sadly scrapes his feet,
And, although stumbling with fatigue,

If on this earth I heard
The rumble of trains
Let my souls revive themselves!

■ It was the night of the twenty-third of March, nineteen thirteen. And if I am going to give minute details on the state of my soul this latter-end-of-winter evening, it is because these hours were the most memorable of my life. I wish also to show the strangenesses of my character, seat of my inconsistencies; my detestable nature, which, nevertheless, I would not exchange for any other, even though it has always hindered me from following a line of conduct; for it makes me sometimes honest, sometimes deceitful, and vain and modest, coarse or distinguished. I want to make you guess them, that you may not detest me, as, presently, you will perhaps feel tempted to do so on reading this.

It was the night of the twenty-third of March, nineteen thirteen.

Without a doubt we are not physically alike, my legs are probably much longer than yours, and my head, highly perched as it is, is happily balanced; our chest measurement differs also, which, probably, will prevent you from weeping and laughing with me.

It was the night of the twenty-third of March, nineteen thirteen. It was raining. Ten o'clock had already struck. I was reposing, dressed, on my bed, and had not taken care to light the lamp, for that evening I felt myself flag before such a great effort. I was frightfully bored. I would say. "Ah, Paris, what hatred I bear you! What are you doing in this city? Ah! that's right! No doubt you think you'll succeed! Why twenty years are necessary for that, my poor man, and if you attain your fame you will then be ugly as a man. I shall never understand how Victor Hugo could, for forty years, pursue his labours. All literature is:

■ **Oscar Wilde Lives!**[16]

ta, ta, ta, ta, ta, ta. Oh, damn it!" — I become terribly coarse at such moments — and yet I feel that I do not surpass the limits, for I stifle in spite of it all. Nevertheless, I aspire to success, for I feel I should know what humorous uses to make of it, and would find it amusing to be famous; but how manage to take myself seriously? To think that, given that we exist, we do not laugh continuously. But — another perplexity — I also wish to lead the marvellous life of the *raté*.[17] And as sadness with me is always mingled with pleasantry, it was "Oh la la's" quickly followed by "tra la la's!" I thought too: I am spending my capital. Great! I can guess what my troubles will be when, towards forty, I shall see myself, from every point of view, ruined. "Oh la!" I would immediately add as a sort of conclusion to these little verses; for it was necessary that I should laugh on. Seeking some amusement, I tried to rhyme, but inspiration, ever ready to tease the will at a thousand turns, completely failed me. By force of racking my brains, I found this quatrain — of a commonplace irony which quickly disgusted me:

> *J'étais couché sur mes draps,*
> *Comme un lion sur le sable,*
> *Et, pour effet admirable,*
> *Je laissais pendre mon bras.*[18]

Incapable of originality, and not renouncing my efforts to create, I sought to add lustre to ancient poems, forgetting that verse is an incorrigible child! Naturally I had no more success: everything remained mediocre. At last — ultimate extravagance — I imagined the *prosopoème*, a thing of the future, the execution of which, moreover, I put off to the happy — and how lamentable — days of inspiration. The idea in view was of a piece begun in prose which, through insensible iterations — rhyme — at first remote then closing in more and more, should give birth to pure poetry.

Then I relapsed into my sad thoughts.

What made it worse was that I was still in Paris, too weak to leave it; that I had an apartment and even furniture — at that moment I could have burnt the house down — that I was in Paris though lions and giraffes exist; and I thought that science herself had begotten mammoths, and that we already saw naught but elephants; and that in a thousand years the reunion of all the machines in the world would cause no more noise than: "scs, scs, scs." This "scs, scs, scs," enlivened me, feebly. I am here, on this bed, like a sluggard; not that it displeases me to be a terrible loafer; but I hate to remain *for long* only that, when our epoch is the most favourable to men of enterprise and to thieves; I, to whom an air on the violin suffices to awaken a madness for life; I who could kill myself through pleasure; die of love for all women; who weeps for every citiy, I am here, *because life has no solution.* I can make merry in Montmartre and a thousand eccentricities, since I need them; I can be pensive, physically; change step by step into sailor, gardener or barber; but, if I want to savour the voluptuousnesses of the priest, I must bestow a lustrum on my forty years' existence, and lose incalculable pleasures, during the time I must remain solely chaste. I, who dream of myself even amid catastrophes, I say that man is only so unfortunate because a thousand souls inhabit a single body.

It was the night of the twenty-third of March, nineteen thirteen. Occasionally I could hear a tug-boat whistle, and would inwardly say: "Why are you so poetic, since you go no farther than Rouen, and do not run any danger? Ah! let me laugh, laugh, but truly laugh, like Jack Johnson!"

No doubt I had, that evening, the soul of a man deceived, for nobody, I am certain — since I have never formed a friend — nobody has loved as much as I: each flower transforms me into a butterfly; more than a ewe, to trample on the grass ravishes me; the air, oh, the air! for entire afternoons have I not occupied myself in breathing? On nearing the sea, does not my heart dance like a buoy? and from the moment I cleave the waves my organism is that of a fish. Amid nature, I feel myself leafy; my hair is green and my blood is green; often, I adore a pebble; the angelus is dear to me; and I love to listen to memory when it whistles plaintively.

I had slipped into my stomach, and must have begun to fall into a fairy-like state; for my digestive tube was suggestive; my mad cells danced; and my shoes seemed to me miraculous. What incites me still more to think thus, is that at that moment I remarked the feeble noise of a bell, the ordinary timbre of which, seemingly, diffused itself through all my members, like some marvellous liquid. I arose slowly and, precipitately, went to open the door, joyous at such an unexpected diversion. I pulled it open; an immense man stood before me.

"Monsieur Lloyd?

—That is me, said I; will you please come in."

And the stranger trod over my doorstep with the magical air of a queen or a pigeon.

"I am going to light up . . . pardon me for receiving you thus . . . I was alone, and . . .

—No, no, no; please, don't in any way trouble yourself."

I insisted.

"Once again, I pray you, said the stranger, receive me in the dark.

Amused, I offered him an arm-chair, and faced him. Immediately he began:

"Can your ears bear to hear things unheard-of?

—Pardon me, I stammered, pardon me, a little shocked. I have not quite understood.

—I said, Can your ears bear to hear things unheard-of?"

This time, I simply said: "yes."

Then, after some moments, he whom I thought a stranger said: "I am Sebastian Melmoth."[19]

Never shall I be able to render what passed within me: in sudden and total self-abnegation, I wanted to fall on him and clasp his neck, to embrace him like a mistress, give him to eat and to drink, put him to bed, dress him, become his procurer, in short, to draw all my money from the bank and fill his pockets. The only words I could succeed in articulating to sum up my innumerable sentiments were: "Oscar Wilde! Oscar Wilde!" The latter understood my trouble and my love, and murmured: "Dear Fabian." To hear myself named thus familiarly and tenderly touched me to the point of tears. Then, my mood changing, I inhaled, like an exquisite perfume, the delight of being one of the actors in a unique situation.

The moment after, a mad curiosity spurred me, to wish that I might distinguish him in the darkness. And, carried away by passion, I did not feel it embarrassing to say:

"Oscar Wilde, I should like to see you; let me light this room.

—Do so," he answered me in a very soft voice.

I went therefore into a neighbouring room to find the lamp, but, by its weight, I knew it to be empty; and it was with a candle that I returned to my uncle.

I immediately looked on Wilde; an old man with white beard and hair, it was he!

An unutterable pain strangled me. Though I had often, in idleness, calculated the age that Wilde should have today, the only image that enchanted me, repudiating even that of the mature man, was that of him youthful and triumphant. What! To have been poet and youth, noble and rich, and now be nothing more than old and sad. Destiny! was it possible? Forcing back my tears and approaching him, I embraced him! I ardently kissed his cheek; then I rested my blond hair on his snowy head, and for a long, long time, I sobbed.

Poor Wilde did not thrust me from him; on the contrary, my head was even softly encircled by his arm; and he pressed me against him. He said nothing, only, once or twice, I heard him murmur: "Oh, my God! oh, my God!" Also, "God has been terrible!" By some strange aberration of the heart, this last word, pronounced with a strong English accent, gave me — though still plunged in my atrocious anguish — a diabolical desire to laugh; and this all the more that, at the same second, a hot tear of Wilde's rolled on my wrist; which gave rise in me to this horrible sally: "The captain's tear!" This jest restored my serenity, and hypocritically detaching myself from Wilde, I went to reseat myself in front of him.

I then commenced to study him. I examined his head first, which was furrowed with profound wrinkles and nearly bald. The thought dominating me was that Wilde seemed more musical than plastic, without wishing to give a very precise sense to this definition; truly, more musical than plastic. I regarded him above all in his ensemble. He was beautiful. In his arm-chair, he had the air of an elephant; he crushed the seat, where he was cramped; before those enormous arms and legs I sought, admiringly, to imagine the divine sentiments possessing such members. I considered the width of his boots; the foot was relatively small, a bit flat, which should have sufficed to give its possessor the cadenced and dreamy dignity of pachyderms, and, thus set up, to mysteriously make a poet of him. I adored him because he resembled a large beast; I pictured him . . . simply, as a hippopotamus, and the image ravished me because of its candour and justice; for without friends of evil influence, he must have hoped for all things from inauspicious climates, and had returned either from the East Indies or Sumatra, or from elsewhere. Very certainly, he had wished to die in the sun — perhaps in Obock — and it is somewhere in those parts that I poetically imagined him, among the riotous greenery of Africa, amid the music of flies, creating mountains of excrement.

What strengthened this idea in me, is that the new Wilde was reserved, and that I had known a postman, equally mute, who might have been an imbecile, but who seemed saved because he had once spent some time in Saigon.

Time abiding, I understood him better on noting his heavy eyes, with the morbid and rare eye-lashes; with eye-balls that seemed to me chestnut, though I should not be able, without lying, to state their veritable colour; and a stare that at no point fixed itself, but spread, like a large cloth. Understanding him better, I could not repel the reflexion: that he was more musical than plastic; and I was surprised that the world should not have sooner come to the opinion that it had before it a lost man.

His bloated visage was diseased; the thick, bloodless lips would at times uncover teeth that were rotten and scrofulous, repaired with gold; a great white and brown beard — I perceived that this last colour, not wishing to admit the white — almost always masked his chin. I pretended that the hairs were silvery, without being so, because there was something as if grilled about them, the clusters they formed seemed tinted with the ardent hues of the skin. It had pushed forth indifferently, in the same manner that time, or Oriental boredom, prolongs itself.

It was only later that I noticed my guest laughed continuously, not with the nervous contraction of Europeans, but in the absolute. Last of all, his dress interested me; I noticed that he wore a black suit, passably old, and I sensed his indifference to his toilette.

A radiant solitaire, that I could not refrain from coveting, gleamed on his left ear, and it gave Wilde a certain aura.

I had been to seek a bottle of cherry brandy in the kitchen, and had already poured several glasses: we were also smoking excessively; I had begun to lose my discretion and to become noisy; it was then that I permitted myself this vulgar question:

"Have they never recognised you?

—Yes, several times, above all at first, in Italy. One day even, in the train, a person seated opposite me gazed at me so intently that I thought it advisable to unfold my newspaper and put it up, so as to escape his curiosity; for I was not unaware that this man knew I was Sebastian Melmoth." Wilde persisted in naming himself thus. "And, what is more frightful, this man followed me when I left the train — I belive it was in Padua — seated himself opposite me in the restaurant, and having, I cannot tell by what means, picked up some acquaintances — for, like me, the man seemed a stranger — he had the horrible pleasantry to cite my poet's name aloud, feigning discourse on my works. And all of them turned, their eyes drilling me, to see if I would falter. Nothing was left me but to quit the town that night. I also came across men whose eyes were deeper than the eyes of other men, and whose glances clearly said: 'I salute you, Sebastian Melmoth!' "

I was prodigiously interested, and added:

"You are alive when all the world thinks you dead; M. Davray,[20] for example, affirmed to me that he had touched you and that you were dead.

—Why, of course I was dead, my visitor answered, with a manner so atrociously natural that I feared for his reason.

—For my part, in my imagination I have always pictured you in the tomb, between two thieves, like Christ!"

I then asked him for particulars about a trinket fixed to his watch-chain, which, he apprised me, was no other than Marie Antoinette's gold key, which once served to open the secret door of the Petit Trianon.

We drank more and more, and observing Wilde, who was becoming singularly cheerful, I got it in my head to intoxicate him; for he now laughed with great guffaws, reversed in his arm-chair.

I continued: "Have you read the pamphlet that André Gide — what an ass — published about you? He has not understood that you were mocking him in the parable ending, more or less thus: 'And this is called the disciple.' Poor devil, he did not take it as meant for him! And later, where he shows both of you on a café terrace, did you take notice of the passage where the old miser hints that he gave you alms? How much did he give you? A louis?

—Five francs," articulated my uncle, irresistibly comic.

I continued:

"Have you entirely given up work?

—Oh no, I have finished my memoirs — My God, how droll! — I still have a volume of verse in preparation, and I've written four theatre pieces . . . for Sarah Bernhardt! he exclaimed, laughing very loud. I love the theatre very much, but I am never really at my ease until my characters are seated and about to converse. — Listen, old man — I was becoming very familiar — I am going to make you a little proposition and, at the same time, to show myself a discreet manager. Here it is: I publish a little literary review, where I have already exploited you — it's beautiful, a *literary* review! — and I shall ask you for one of your books, which I will publish as a posthumous work; but, if you prefer, I become your impresario; I immediately sign you a contract for a lecture tour in the music halls. If speaking bores you, I shall exhibit you in exotic dances, or in pantomime, with chorus girls."

Wilde was more and more amused. Then, suddenly melancholy, he said: "And Nelly?" (My mother.) This question caused in me a bizarre physical effect because, had they not half informed me of my mysterious birth, several times very vaguely intimating that Oscar Wilde might be my father? I recounted all I knew about her; I even added that Mme. Wilde, before dying, had visited him in Switzerland. I spoke to him of M. Lloyd — my father? — calling to his attention the jest he had made about him: "He is the most insipid [*plat*] man I have ever met." Contrary to my expectations, this memory caused Wilde some chagrin.

I recounted, with respect to Vyvyan and my own family, what was most likely to interest him; but soon I perceived that he was no longer with me.

He had interrupted me but once, during my long discourse, becoming emphatic, when I described my hatred of Swiss scenery. "Yes, he punctuated, how can they like the Alps? For me the Alps are nothing more than great photographs in black and white. When I'm alone among high mountains, I feel myself crushed; I lose all sense of my personality; I am no longer myself; my sole desire is to get away. When I descend into Italy, little by little, I find myself once more: I become a man again."

As the conversation had dropped off, he resumed: "Tell me about yourself."

I then made him a picture of my adventurous life: I gave him a thousand details of my childhood, the terror of all the schools and institutions of Europe; of my hazardous life in America; the anecdotes multiplied; and Wilde would cease laughing gaily only to enjoy, in convulsions, every situation in which my charming instincts came to light. And it was "Oh dear, oh dears," continuously.

The bottle of cherry brandy was empty, and the rowdy was gradually born in me.

I brought out three litres of *vin ordinaire*, the only beverage remaining; but, when I offered it to my new friend, the latter, much swollen, made a gesture of refusal with his hand.

"*Come on! Have a bloody drink!*"[21] I exclaimed, in an American boxer's accent, at which he seemed a little shocked; "Good Lord, I have killed your dignity."

He accepted, nevertheless, emptied his glass at a gulp, and sighed; "In all my life, I have never drunk so much."

—Shut up, old souse!" I yelled, pouring another drink. Then, breaking all bounds, I began to interrogate him as follows: "Old carcass! will you tell me right off where you come from? How did you happen to know which floor I live on?" And I shouted: "Hurry up and answer; are you still at the faking stunt? Oh no, really, I'm not your father! And insulting him with abominable belching: "Hey! Piss off! You street-corner whore, good-for-nothing, plug-ugly shit-shovel scrapings, cottager, imbecile, old queen, whacking great cow . . !"

I'm not sure whether Wilde savoured these splendid pleasantries, in which wit had gone the whole hog, so to speak — an easy trick, and one which permits one to preserve, amid the most apparent trivialities, all one's nobility. No doubt that evening I did not wish to refrain from

a certain coquetry of manner; for, in such cases, the elegance that I
have described depends only upon the intention, something so simple
that it will always attract a juggler of etiquette, though he be well
aware of the whole price of mere vulgarity.

Be that as it may, Wilde remarked, laughing:

"How amusing you are! But, Aristide Bruant, what ever became of
him?" Which immediately called up in my mind: "You've said it,
Charles, now you've put your foot in it, you old bloater!"[22]

At a certain moment my visitor even ventured: "*I am dry.*"[23] Which
can be translated thus: "*Je suis sec.*" And I filled his glass again. Then,
with an immense effort, he arose, but I promptly flattened him — this
is the precise term — on his armchair with a shove of my fore-arm.
Without protest he pulled out his watch: it was a quarter of three.
Forgetting to consult him first, I shout: "To Montmartre! We shall go
on a spree." Wilde seems unable to resist, and his face shines with joy;
nevertheless, he says weakly:

"I can't, I can't.

—I am going to take you round the bars and bore you; there, I shall
pretend to lose you, and will cry out, very loud: 'Oscar Wilde, come
have a whiskey. You'll see, we shall be astonishing! and you will
thereby prove that society has availed nothing against your fine
organism.' " And I said again, like Satan"Besides, are you not the King
of Life?"

—You are a terrible boy, murmured Wilde in English. My God! I
should like to, but I can't; really, I can't. I implore you, do not try a
tempted soul thus. I am going to leave you, Fabian, and now I bid you
goodbye."

I no longer opposed his departure; and, standing, he shook hands
with me, took his hat, which he had placed on the table, and made for

the door. I accompanied him down the stairs, and, somewhat more lucid, asked:

"By the way, did you not come here on some mission?

—No, none, keep silent on all you have heard and seen . . . or rather, say whatever you like in six month's time."

On the side-walk he pressed my fingers, and embracing me whispered again: "*You are a terrible boy.*"24

I watched him disappear into the night, and as life, at that moment, forced me to laugh, I stuck my tongue out at him, and mimicked the action of giving him a good hard kick.

It was no longer raining, but the air was cold. I remembered that Wilde had no overcoat, and I told myself he must be poor. A gush of sentiment inundated my heart; I was sad and full of tenderness; seeking some consolation, I lifted my eyes: the moon was too beautiful and increased my pain. I thought now that Wilde had perhaps wrongly interpreted my words; that he had not understood that I could not be *serious*; that I had caused him pain. And, like a madman, I started to run after him; at each corner, I sought him with all the strength of my eyes and shouted: "Sebastian! Sebastian!" Full speed, I raced through the boulevards until I realised that I had lost him.

Wandering through the streets, I returned slowly, and my eyes never left the moon, companionable as a curse.

■ **Poet and Boxer**

■ Whoo-eee! Off to America in 32 hours. Only been back in London from Bucharest two days before bumping into the man I was after: the one who would meet all the expenses of a six-month tour. No contract, of course! Not that I gave a damn about that. After all, it wasn't as if I was about to dump my wife!!! Shit! And you'll never guess what I had to do: put on exhibition fights under the pseudonym of *The Mysterious Sir Arthur Cravan*, the world's shortest-haired poet, *Grandson of the Chancellor to the Queen*, of course, *Oscar Wilde's Nephew*, likewise of course, and *Alfred Lord Tennyson's Great Nephew*, once again of course (I'm wising up now). The fights were to be something completely new: Tibetan rules, the most scientific known to man and even more terrible than jiu-jitsu — the slightest pressure on a single nerve or tendon, no matter which, and splat! your opponent (who was absolutely not bribed, well maybe a little bit) falls to the ground like a man struck by lightning! If that doesn't crack you up, how about this: by my reckoning this will really bring the money rolling in and if everything goes according to plan I should make some 50,000 francs out of the deal, which isn't to be sniffed at. In any event, it was much better than the spiritualism racket that I'd been working.

I was 17 years old and sitting pretty and I went back — along with a pair of wasters who had nothing better to do, one a sort of painter and the other some kind of poet (tum-te-tum-te-bum-hole) who were full of admiration for me (what a joke!) and who had been boring me stiff for the last hour recounting anecdotes about Rimbaud, free verse, Cézanne, Van Gogh, oh Jesus, Renan (I think) and Christ knows what else — to the hotel to give the news to my other half in the hope of getting something out of her.

I found Mrs Cravan on her own, and I told her what had happened even as I was packing my trunks, for there wasn't a minute to lose. In common time, and in three movements, I folded my silk hosiery, 12 frs. a pair, which put me on a par with Raoul the Butcher, and my shirts on which the remains of the dawn still lingered. The following morning, I bestowed on my lawfully wedded wife my mottled one-piece fishing-rod and handed her five crisp 100 fr. abstractions. Then I went off to take a giant leak. That evening, I scraped a few sad melodies on my fiddle, kissed my baby's kiss-curl, and was all lovey-dovey with the kids. Then, waiting for the off, and dreaming of my stamp collection, I clumped up and down on my elephant's feet with my nose in the air savouring the omnipresent and utterly charming aroma of farts. 6.16 p.m. Vroom! Down the stairs! Straight into a taxi. It was time for aperitifs. The moon, as bloated as a million, presented a fair analogy with a digested rheumatism tablet. I was thirty-four and in my prime. I had folded my six foot frame into the back of a taxi where my knees stuck out in front of me like a pair of polished globes, and I noticed how the paving-stones reflected rainbows of garnet-red gristle criss-crossed with green beefsteaks; how flakes of gold dusted the iridescent trees, the solar nucleus of transfixed bipeds; and, lastly, the passers-by of the adored sex with their pink fringes and buttocks like sentimental landscapes and, from time to time, amongst the greatest shit-hot pains in the arse, I could see a flock of resplendent phoenixes arise.

My impresario was waiting for me as agreed on platform 8 at the station and I immediately warmed to his familiar vulgarity, his veal-stew cheeks which I'd already tasted before, his hair pullulating yellow and vermilion, his beetle-like brain, and, near the right temple, a mole of singular charm as well as the radiating pores of his golden clock.

I found a corner in a First Class compartment and made myself comfortable. That is to say I let down my guard and stretched out my legs in the most casual manner in the world.

And under my lobster skull I juggled my World Champion's orbs
So as to survey the crowd, assembled almost by accident,
When I spotted a gent, an apothecary or a solicitor,
Who smelled like a janitor or a pelican.
Ha! Ha! This I liked: his proclivities
Revealed themselves much as they do with a herbivore,
While his head reminded me quite strongly
Of the time when I used to curl up for the night beside my dumb-bell,
And, I'm bound to say, with a sort of very real adoration
Not to mention something difficult to explain
In the presence of the polished egoist
Whom I bottled with my Atlantic eyes,
I worshipped his forearm as a sacred dish
And compared his stomach to the attraction of shops.
Tickets, please!

Christ Almighty! I'm sure that 999 people out of 1,000 would have had their gustation completely ruined by the voice of the inspector. I'm quite convinced of this, and yet I can confess in all sincerity that it caused me not the slightest inconvenience. On the contrary, in the homogenous compartment the timbre of his voice had the musical qualities of the chirping of little birds. The beauty of the bench-seats was, if anything, enhanced to such a degree that I began to wonder if I

was not the victim of the beginnings of a motor disorder, especially as
I was still staring at that beastly little bourgeois, the tenderest of arse-
holes as ever lived, while wondering what on earth was so fascinating
about the heavy-weight sitting opposite me who seemed to be soundly
asleep. I was thinking: never has moustache emanated such an intense
corporeality and, above all, My God how I love you:

And while allophagous[25]
In the glow of your loving,
Our tangled
Waistcoats entwine,
My darling cauliflower,
I follow your vast range
And your colours,
And in an amalgam
Of Jack Johnson, elephant-seal and wardrobe
Our turds glisten like watered silk.
Fuck-fuck! The beat
Of the breeches
In the final
Abdominal
Spasm!

"Property-owners are termites," I exclaimed suddenly, hoping to
wake the old buffer up, of whom I'd had it up to here, and give him a
start. Then, looking him in the whites of the eyes, once more: "You
heard right. I'll say it again at the risk of getting myself locked up: by
the beard of the nanny-goat and the whiskers of the she-rat, property-
owners are *term-mites!*" From the astonished look on his face, I could

see that he took me for a madman or a fearful ruffian, but he pretended not to understand, so afraid was he that I'd give him a knuckle sandwich. Stupid of me really, especially with my mentality, not to have noticed an American lady and her daughter sitting almost on top of me. It was only when the mother made off for the loo that I paid any attention to them, and in a sentimentive sense I went off with her.

My mind flickered idly from her purse to her sorrows.
And when she resumed her seat, I eyed up her earrings and thought
                                                     how beautiful she was
with her money and, despite her wrinkles and her ageing carcass:
She is not altogether lacking in charm
              for a heart guided by self-interest which does not give a toss
about anything provided there is some advantage to be had. And I told
myself angrily:
Rrrr! Fancy dragging yourself to the porcelain for a jerk off, you bitch!
I'll give you what you're after, you old slut!

What is so funny about all this, not to mention typical of me, is that I came round to turning my attention to the youngest, this is after racking my brains for a way of conning mumsy out of her worldly possessions; it must be in my evil nature, and dreaming of sharing a nice bourgeois existence with her. I assure you that it's true and that I couldn't help thinking: "My dear fellow, what a queer fish you are. You could completely reform me, little girl. Ah! If only you would marry me! I'll show you every kindness and consideration, we would roam the world buying happiness but we'll live in a chic hotel in San Francisco. I don't give a damn about my impresario (not that the daft

sod has an inkling either). We'll spend entire afternoons loving each
other on drawing-room divans, heads down, thighs apart. On your
merest whim, we'll ring for the maid. Flames will leap from the carpets
before our eyes, can you see them,

The valuable paintings, the heavy furniture:
The buhl cabinets and the symmetrical dressers,
With blushing underbellies,
Will stuff to bursting our golden organs.
The paralytic walls,
Secreting sapphires,
Will execute gymnastic movements
Of ibises and tapirs;
On bewitched ottomans
With our palmed feet,
We shall rest our heavy pectorals
And purringly
Savour
Our tongues superior to oysters
And silently fart satin into velvet.
As with pasta, banal thoughts
Will stuff us like geese,
As belly pressed to belly,
Stronger than two shoes,
Emanating a liverish warmth all the while,
Will bathe in their intestinal auroras."
"I say, boy, here we are: Liverpool." It was my manager speaking.
"Allllright."

■ Had I known Latin at eighteen, I would have been Emperor —
Which is more nefarious: the climate of the Congo or genius? —
vegetable patches (carrots) in the shape of a tomb — thoughts jump
out of the fire — stars, the despair of poets and mathematicians —
more virginal and more furious — does it not suffice for a man of
discipline in need of a change to sit at the other end of his study table
once a month — for a moment I thought of signing this Arthur the
First — I rise with the milkmen — in my verdant towers — dog-flesh
— white frost, hoar-frost — O my heart! O my forehead! (O my
veins!) whichever of the two of us that has the most quicksilver in his
veins (syphilis) — I ran my tongue over their eyes (women) — the
moon was drinking, the sea was... the gilded moon — I shall eat my
shit — the Eiffel Tower more gentle than a fern — one clearly feels
the instrument is there (speaking of the heart) — forests and sawmill
— energy — concerning the dust of emperors, I have had it in my eyes
— I will not tolerate people treading on my toenail — our limbs are
already borne by the air (aviation) — if I could amble — the serious
hour (evening) — the sea of blue hair — the movement of the mist —
I have dreamed of being great enough to found and fashion a republic
all to myself — I have dreamed of a bed which would float on water
and, more vulgarly, of sleeping on tigers — I haunt paths — I would
follow the movement of mist on the theatre of the plains and valleys
where the rectangular plantations of radishes and cabbages seemed to
form vast tombs — electro-semaphore — *I would stare at the sea* from
twenty metres above — pigs [?] shake off torpor — my soul ... takes
its place on the pavements — the Romanesque also of an English
nature — telegrams — the blue water of the rain, the downpour —

the dusty ladybirds of museums — its snows on empty benches — the greatest monuments create the most dust — all these fruits are promised to the autumn — all that glitters in the spring is promised to winter — the silver sun of winter — Canada, I know that you are green — and take a stroll in the woods! — the dust of Caesars is raised by the wind — what am I, where are ... and my books of love? the universal vessel — freshen the roses — (à propos the war) I would be ashamed to let myself be carried away by Europe — let her die, I don't have the time — far from my brothers and far from the balloons — I love her, her manner of today is filled with genius, while I find her manner of yesterday visionary, and as for that of the day before yesterday... — what I like about myself ... I have twenty countries in my memory and I drag the colours of a hundred cities in my soul — the Persian nightingale who whistles for his rose — on the ships of Asia and the gentle elephants — my pen trembles and quivers — I am always moved — reading my books is dangerous for the body — the majority of women will sigh — fatty brain, a mind which scratches glass — my thoughts like boas — we moderns, what we have in our hearts is enough to blow up a fortress — the sun reddens Russia — the sublime lamp of the sun — regions rich in oil — and all the stars spin and revolve with silent transmissions — let me fly far away following your traces — am I somewhere — withdrawn under in my verdant towers — the moving stars sing like a limousine — I withdraw under the ferns — at the foot of the pines — what am I not in the fields! — ... and I come to you on a beautiful ocean liner — Until when? How long will I dally at ... ? — phantoms of railway stations — *embouchure* — far from the balloons, virile — colonial — the spirit of independence — current account — enthusiasm — good-bye the passions   of a twenty year old! in the dry season —

nickel —

Boredom — tarnishes my cells — The follies of the eccentric April moon — Big boy — my blond hair, colonist, far from the balloons — established under the planks — In blond Maryland   and far from the balloons   of my little finger — I fight for breath *equally* (also) grit — my heart, break into a gallop — I feel the verses swimming in the dampness of my brain — I'm ruined, fantasy, madness has lost its dancer — vagabond — temperament — Honest, I know myself for the creature and thief that I am — My heart, break into a gallop, I will be a millionaire — I wake up a Londoner and go to bed an Asiatic — Londoner, monocle — furore and fury — O, you who have known me follow me into life — The wind excites me — I am always nervous — I have put on again my belt of scrupulous   , I have dedicated myself to life, I am in good shape — rippling muscles — aristocratic salons — vases and medals — Greek — principally — pretubercular — I have also been the poet of destinies — voltaic arcs — inter-digital space — multifloral rose-bushes — samples — quantity — room, vase of air, atmosphere, intoxicating oxygen — rich and poor, money has made me taste rare boredom and fresh desire — in my soul I drag piles of locomotives, cracked columns, scrap-iron — pseudo-Lloyd, golden plume — so-called — ogling eyes — the hollow wheat lifts its head, Napoleon lowers his — here are the child, the man and the woman ... — happy to have been born — happy by biological necessity — Victor Hugo, the greatest verse-making machine of the nineteenth century — cast up on the coast of Japan — the ephemeral has deep roots in me — the thick and thin are *at war inside me* — Lord, chastity consumes us — breath of springtime, I breathe like a whale — every time I set eyes on someone who is better dressed than myself I am shocked — tell me where you live that in following your traces I might fly as far — the queens of the aquarium (fish) — how beautiful is the snow, the good Lord did not make fun of us — two hearts, four brains, pink colossus and mirror of the world and poetry machine — my swimming days — there is no risk of the Cubists setting fire to their canvases as they paint them — seated like a guitar player — I am enough of a brute to give myself a smack in the teeth and subtle to the point of neurasthenia — man, pensioner, young girl, child and baby — abstract and rascally — I bet that there is not a Chilean nor an *Obokian* in the world who can say to me: "Because of the colour of my skin and my size I once felt something that you could not have felt" — Just let anyone come up to me and say such a thing and I'll spit in his eye — my art which is the most difficult because I adore it and I shit on it — eyes of a woman, neck of a bull — great laggard — viper and duck — his teeth, freshly seen to, sparkled in his mouth like golden statues — the lions are dead — and all the same when I give you elevators of gold — rhinoceroses, fat boilers, my brothers in thickness — when the sun dies in the woods — the maddest of the mad is me — and I look at you, all you specialists — my God! when I think that I'm thirty years old, it drives me wild — I like my bed because it is the only place where I can play possum, pretending to be dead while all the time breathing like the living — when I go on a binge, I can hear the voice of dictionaries — ... if all the locomotives in the world began screeching at the same time they could not express my anguish — I am perhaps the king of failures, because I'm certainly the king of something — *the same while changing* — I go to ... the spheres ... — athletic melancholy —

Support thought — dreaming of Saturn — I already aspire to other readers — I don't give a damn about art yet if I had known Balzac I would have tried to steal a kiss from him — the heart discovers and the head invents —

Breasts, elephants of softness — in the name of God the shit, the bitch, the decaying carcass — my heart in its passion embraces the age of stone — Nature, I am your servant — Nero of the pit — It is time to sing from the depths of my heart — torrents of memories — heart of hearts — off you go, little specialists — I do furiously ... — chimera of springtime — and change shirts — my whinnying youth — dead blacks — in the air purified by the volcanoes — blond colossus, blond giant — fleas breed on eagles, cretins in palaces — and to the para-infernal belongings of a woman — Philadelphia — line, service — I have known the happiness of ...

Farewell, sovereign fern of the Eiffel Tower ... love, April, perched on step-ladders — behind the factories — locomotive boilers — Venus in the gardens — a binge of curtains — lungs — Really electro-semaphores! cyclists, connecting-rods — traffic of skins — intense — external — epidermis — ... shone on the facade of stations — play in Maryland — as far as, in the roots of eyes — smoke, I see your spirals — no artist has ever been found hanging before a rose — oxygen, I feel pink — vigils ... factories — throw pebbles — verses carried nine years like the elephant — no body, do you understand, no body ... — dirtied by the sun — why do actors not recite Latin and Greek verse? the pasture of the moon — when dawn changes the dress of glaciers — the adopted, adoptive green — in the farms —

In the sombre beauty of a darkening cloud

The moon that dreamed like an elephant's heart

The Saint-Laurent under the yoke of bridges — I noticed that female servants minister to M. Gide's chastity — verses carried nine years like the elephant and died seven times in the waves of the heart — chimneys, smoke, smoke, my beautiful dishevelled ones! — my black death, funereal images, your *finery*, in the kingdom of death, moles will furnish you, my sister, yet more *fur* — ... your territorial waters —

Ah, in the name of God, what weather and what a spring — palm-trees and towers — manufacture — ... like a beautiful charcoal-burner — ... and I love your presidents — I miss masterpieces — I come freshly to admire your houses — It is me, your Cravan

wind

I feel the bloom of my youth and come fresh-faced
To admire America and its new cycle-racing tracks
My noble nature — astride a bicycle —
What is there really in your heart, melancholy ogre?
Where does it come from this shadow,
The regard of a beautiful female charcoal-burner?
I want no more of these sinister pleasures.
And you, winter sun whom I love to madness
   you live in a child
   and surprise in passing
In the sombre beauty of a darkening cloud
The moon that dreamed like an elephant's heart.

For five years now you have not been the same, I do not wish to grow old — court purveyor — my elector's card — ... I swear to you — poet-woodcutter — honour — extravagantly — the genius which consumes a kilo of flesh a week — weekly — obesity of the heart, fullness of figure — around 200 frs., my heart shows a credit, bank — the total — literally mad — ... to have a great deal of hope — You place lakes under the yoke of bridges — I study death through my portholes — Tarnished street-lamps — naval spirit — to reiterate —

I am a man of heart, and am sure to be such;

However...   (hotels)

The past bellowed like a bull — the air in my wind-pipe — ... make his propellers hum — ... like a white automobile — young dumb-bellophile — *A Curse on My Muse* — *love* on its scaffolding — the colporteur — temperature — in short — tramp! — Franco-Britannic — postal order —

Glorification of scandal (the municipality of New York) — eternal April (tenor) perched on its scaffolding and how cold everything one says is in comparison — Wit has its facets and the soul (the heart) has its slopes — my passports — vulgarity — demoralised — at the hour one turns the lights on in offices — street-lamps shine on their grounded stars — Porto-Rico — the olive-tree falls asleep again — elephant prophet — my leg play —

Sovereign fern of the Eiffel
Tower.

I am everything and every inundation — after crying able to tear up my tears — I need a tremendous spree of debauchery — I am the child of my epoch — organism —

I am what I am: the baby of an epoch. My heart shaken like a bottle — to pass with the utmost speed from enthusiasm to the most complete demoralisation —

I am the beautiful Flora, *Laurent* de Médicis

My thoughts are sweet — creature — by killing thought — the savant, the smell of the wind — furore and fury — the father of butterflies — I love eyes: tennis, ... football, prairie billiards — My stomach illuminates a salon, thieves' delight —

When I dream of ... the blood of conquerors goes to my head —

What have your tiny contradictions got to do with me? — Springtime in the branches — Syphilitic atlas — Lord, Lord, am I declining? and my swimming days — yesterday your memory caused me a sickly dream — the corset of roses — carcass, diamonds, stones of sexual attraction — leaf tobacco — Charente, your branches and moss — star of the Equator — the past has dark eyes, the future a gilded plumage — descriptive ornithology — organs, luminous larvae — alas and hurrah! — petrifications — I turn over the memory of broken boilers — my horse-like belly — don't forget to go — gold or bull — I will stamp on you, fatality — but where is the monument to my robberies, jokes? — art, painting have betrayed me — wome 's delicate organs — I rest my legs on moss — What sort of weather do you want painting, and what demands do you make? Desires, you have left me slumped half-dead in a chair — possession — A fearsome laziness — I romp on the lawn — receive the insult of a chosen one — the crystal of the moon — romance of fighters — the fruit of a Negress — my resplendent feet, their splendour — Model of injustice — the wit of the ruse — treasure of burglars, of the worldly — thousand and one — pillar of madness —

                              amidst the detritus of the years

    I turn over the memory of broken boilers — charming polypods — I burden the walls with my presence — Rimbaud's verses whistle by — I shall see the Woolworths which is so large that one is unable to tell when walking around lower Broadway if one is walking around it or if it is walking around us — land of space when I will sleep in your overcoat — the laws of art remain, the rules are superseded — My gardener's heart — The moment he sits on a bench the wickedest man or the greatest drunk turns into a judge — You cannot understand, I am Musset, Beethoven, the one who pulled the job in the rue des Reculettes — the prosodist with measured feet, the poet with the gait of the bear —

On the benches of the square
amongst strange victims
The poet sits down equal to those with amputated limbs —
Atlas without a world,   overburdened
Never speak to me again of influence, I have always wondered what
I have to do to cut a dash — The death of the greatest of men is
incapable of even stopping a train — Remember that my weight has
often been my despair — turbulent — the moon serves as my
entourage — my homework — I am not a pig — with my burning
genius I was on time — my Renée, when you are dying — by boat to
Baltimore — chimera of springtime, ghosts of autumn — What world
of sadness conceals the calm of my heart? — in the sky, harbourer of
winds — stifling, elephant — That I could leap into the grass of
springtime — The only criticism that one may make of these
paintings is that one has no desire to embrace the artist — jewelleries
— frantic assassin — the creation — at bottom I am ... The
darkening sun over the still warm sun — Manicure, give me my days
of autocracy, my morale and my taste — ... inferior shows — What a
sensation I have caused sometimes — I burden the walls with my
presence like a *corps d'amour* — What is it? The torrent sings, the tiger
roars and the fir-tree rustles? — gigantic hearts — if I belie Christ and
Wagner —
Amidst the rubble of the years
I turn over the memory of broken boilers
— my thousand hearts are yours — parallelograms — an inanimate
smile — ... and the tooth of the lion — gloomy and petrified —
maternal cabbages — in my dreams columns of cars move forward —
often when night comes the thief awakens — Ah! However great you
are there are many who have never heard of you — the dreamer as

masturbator — I govern my eyes as if they were kingdoms — love faster than the post — My poor Gorve — Why do you call me poor? — Because you are part of the world — life is not worth the trouble of being lived, but I am worth living for — and it is not for irises that I have such irises of my own — few understand that you have to be a mason or a Russian prince to eat a steak with your fingers and even fewer understand what it takes to be vulgar — My happiness is not in my head but in my youth — tyrannical God — Everyone has a secret idea of God, just as everyone has a cabinet — the mathematician shaken by gas — it is dangerous for the body to dream too long — if I have a genius it is an exclusively humorous one, and I indisputably have a genius, and affirm that one often sees genius (the highest faculty to which man may attain, according to the dictionary) that cannot be conceived of! — God, what an imbecile! —

Churches   your chaste music
Submitting   to the laws of physics
force the secretaries — removals I... — Why do you love me? — Part of the job — I desire furiously that he is liked — And why, if you please? — In order that you notice him and so revive the languishing conversational sallies — Your eyes strike me like agates mounted in a golden talon of eyelashes (O, the counter-stratagems of delinquency!)

Brrm, brrm, brrm, brrm!!! What meaning do you give to these broum, broum, broums? — My dear Miss, my dear individual of a state of mind so unclassifiable that it is impossible to find its expression in spoken language. It is of the first importance, moreover, not to mistake them for a boudi boum bada boum — How amusing you are — I am quite serious, but by perversity... whatever you like. Tell me though where you come from, where you are going, your age, your weight, how much pocket money you are given and your social position — when anvils open their wings — I shall never amount to much. My parents neglected to give me a religious education — Why didn't you come when I called? — Pure ideas are not compelling — Attitude is dead — I understand myself better since I see everyone else — I feel that the walls are reaching their maturity — If one put Goethe in charge of the universe, the stars would soon start to behave erratically — the wall's charms — I have a good stature — I am strong by inspiration and I have an almost unexpected vocation to sing — and my weight is subject to tremendous fluctuation, my friends will tell you as much, my fleshy face becoming drawn in a matter of hours — When the gardener and the man of the world both agree at the same time that I have only one mouth I make a kind of grimace — I just have to laugh when 2 or 3 individuals start, as occasionally happens, to speak at the same moment and I shall explain why at some length. For example, a young man who was showing me some verse written by a girl whom he loved made me laugh by bringing out the sceptic and the romantic in me, the manner in which he reproached me causing me to laugh all the louder because of the appearance of the ruffian and finally to break into paroxysms of laughter at the entrance of the superior ruffian — I distrust him: he weighs the same as ten years ago — I am greatly afraid that his feet have no antipodes — I blush with pleasure — the man of wit: one who knows how to fight in his night-shirt — the brain as muscular as a bull — the litter of stars — (I like) I sit with... — I feel reborn to a life of lies — to set my body to music — to stuff my boxing-gloves with women's earrings — God is barking, we should open the door — I was walking amongst brutes — locomotive, Venus of the forests sleep beside the graminaceae (chimneys) — Maid, Venus, lily-of-the-vestibule — Lord, my beard is like rank weeds and my feet stink — stronger ...

stronger than departure — *adieu* New York, I have only been passing through — The bone-structure of countries forms the topography of bones — in boredom I am both herbivorous and carnivorous — on what should I base my system of the world: a blade of grass or the boxer's thighs? — New York... millions of madmen — I ditched myself in Santiago — Don't forget to telephone — When the rays of the machinery have influenced my head as much as those of the sun — I am ashamed to be white: a white is not even a Negro's corpse — I am going to Buenos Aires to be unhappy — memories dilated by beer — this cephalo-pimp — I reflect on the evolution of the stomach in New York — I am a caressing madman — my thief-like pupil reflects the cat's shining claws — and the mock-traditional brick — the painter who only uses primary colours is like the writer who is forever shouting shit — dream-machine — I follow the moon and I watch it become American — time passes like a giant — the action of the sun — dancing bottles and barrels — no one understands me except myself — and how are you after each time it rains (death) — seeds of music — I no longer sleep — in this hamlet where it is impossible to steal anything — Her cheeks reflect nothing — this young man looks responsible — these young people are late — my hatred of work — the intoxication of love is the same as that of tobacco — to be assimilated with a cigarette — if you see me as an angel of the seamy side of life every time I darn a sock — there are times when I would like to see mothers drop their babies — I entertain some prejudices at last — I contribute my head and my life — a complete man — Lord, I am your equal — treasures of brutality — your blond giant — a mother and a father, what a blemish! — I have advanced so far that I am still afraid of being crushed in the street — I inspire confidence — I shall be gross to rest from the ideal — I must change my mind by listening to a lot of music — I amuse myself madly — I am the incarnation of the furniture and the gamblers — Tell me something interesting — Madame (something extraordinarily profound mixed with something of a Parisian triviality and my personal joke) — the stage of the lines on the hand — I immerse myself in the gold of my watch — as with a pearl I know how to create the orient for myself: I go into a museum of natural history where I shall see the mouldings of the Parthenon — Cravan, Golpeador — give me your nose — If you refuse, I will throw myself under the moon's chariot — she breathes like a cabbage — with painters, painting is a secretion — amongst educated folk almost only the rich are poor — I have my own accent when speaking foreign languages: I was born fair-haired and I gradually become dark-haired — this book undoubtedly has its place amongst present-day overproduction — one should call one's future into question once a year — I watched with a smile the man whose weight had not changed a kilo in ten years — it only remains for me to sell my skeleton to a naturalist or my soul to a psychologist —

languor of elephants, romance of boxers.

■ The atmosphere of New York during the years 1915-1918 was heavily charged as a result of the unusual gathering together of individuals of all nationalities, each of whom had his own reticences and mysteries.

It also turned out to be an exceptionally favourable climate for the development of a certain revolutionary spirit in the domain of the arts and letters which, later on, became crystallized in Europe under the name of Dada.

This spirit, the germs of which were perceptible quite some time before the war, appeared, at first, to be the natural reaction of one generation to the preceding one (in this case, to the rubbish and vanity of the Romantic and Symbolist epochs, through a return to simpler, more natural values).

It was destined to go beyond the limits of aesthetics, to grow venomous, and become charged with blasphemy and harshness under the pressure of events. At a time when society refused the right of existence to every being whom it had not incorporated within its warring exigencies, this spirit became, in an indirect form, a protest, the only possible protest, of persecuted individualism.

It was to manifest itself with unforeseen violence, thanks to the presence in the United States at that time, of Marcel Duchamp and Picabia, who possess, each in his own way, a veritable genius for perturbation and polemics. Looking at it from a vantage-point of twenty years, their systematic plan of disturbance and demoralisation went definitely beyond mere artistic discussions and, in a more general

■ **Witness:** *Arthur Cravan and American Dada* by **Gabrielle Buffet-Picabia**

□ Gabrielle Buffet-Picabia (1881-1985) was married to Francis Picabia with whom she is pictured above. She was active in Paris and New York Dada.

way, assailed the security of all commonplaces, all collective and official hypocrisies.

Scandal and malicious humour were the usual formulae of their manifestations and publications. And so it happened that the Exhibition of Independent Painters, which took place in New York in 1917, became known as a result of several vexatiously sensational incidents. First of all, Marcel Duchamp sent a urinal, signed by him, for exhibition. The jury hesitated a few minutes over whether to consider it as one of those "ready-made masterpieces," which he classifies and catalogues as "masterpieces," by virtue of his choice and signature alone.

The second incident, and not the least, was the lecture given during the exhibition itself by Arthur Cravan, a man who personified, within himself and without premeditation, all the elements of surprise to be wished for in a demonstration that had not yet been christened "Dada."

His appearance alone created a kind of awe. This Cravan, whose real name was Fabian Lloyd, boxer and poet interchangeably, was over six feet tall; his extremely heavy body, admirably proportioned according to its own exceptional measures, bore an olympian head of striking regularity, although somewhat indescribable. Through his mother, he was the nephew of Oscar Wilde, a fact about which he liked to boast, even under circumstances where such a relevation could only be shocking: as for instance, when he enumerated his titles and qualifications before a boxing match. Speaking perfect English, French and German he possessed a British culture of the best type, and was equally familiar with the spirit of Montparnasse, of Montmartre and even more far-flung boulevards. In Paris, he lived among a circle of poets and painters, and he published poems which reveal an undeniable poetic vein, in which he frees himself, by means of a rhythmic argot that is often very moving, of his immoderate and, essentially, rather juvenile aspirations. But he was also on intimate terms with the boxing world, whose society, according to him, he preferred, and he was prouder of his athletic performances than of his literary works.

Above all, however, he proclaimed his incapacity to live according to the social order and its accepted exigencies and he boasted openly that he had successfully accomplished "the perfect burglary": an exploit that had taken place in a Swiss jewellery-store.

From 1912 to 1915 he published, in Paris, under the name of *Maintenant*, a little polemical magazine which was certainly the forerunner of *391*[27] and other aggressive post-war publications. It served as his loud-speaker with which to make known to artists (lest any should be unaware) what he thought of them. His conclusions were often surprising. Van Dongen, alone, found grace in his eyes. But he was not always wrong, and his account of a visit to André Gide, for example, is an extraordinary piece of ironically clever criticism. The article devoted to the Independents Exhibition in Paris in 1914 made him famous, and unleashed a tempest of protests. He attacked the most outstanding names. The women painters, no less than the men, were the object of his insolent commentaries, which were all the more irritating as they were characterized by an irresistible verve and drollery. And although everybody said it was outrageous, they could barely control their chuckles. But he did go too far, nonetheless. It was too evident that he was sure of the impunity which his six feet in height and his athletic shoulders conferred upon him. Those who were insulted, it must be said, did not cut a very brilliant figure, either, when they made a little group of ten or twelve — union makes strength —

and waited for him before the Independents Gallery, where he had come to sell copies of his review, like a news-vendor. The encounter ended at the police station, not to Cravan's advantage. Apollinaire, who loved duels, could not allow this opportunity to pass him by and sent his seconds to the brazen offender of Marie Laurençin. Cravan made obviously hypocritical excuses and everything was all right again.

The declaration of war in 1914 found him in France. He was, of course, quite determined not to answer the call of his native land, and there began an extraordinary series of adventures around his chameleon-like nationalities. No longer is it "little intellectuals with big heads and muscleless legs" with whom he has to match his strength, but with the pitiless police of the warring nations. At last here is a game worth the candle. In 1914 he is a "Swiss subject". We find him in Barcelona in 1916 where he arrived finally, after a long roundabout trip through Central Europe. How had he succeeded in eluding the vigilance of several frontiers? In crossing three or four belligerent countries without being either found out or arrested? And all this without any apparent or normal source of income? Unheard-of adventures that one would have liked to make him recount, but which he kept to himself, for he talked little, as a rule. His manners were extremely reserved and courteous, when he was not drunk. Now the woman who had shared his Paris days came to join him. He proved to be a faithful lover and revealed almost bourgeois virtues. I must add, through having experienced it later on, that he could be a devoted friend, anxious to help and to be counted on. But alcohol liberated alarmingly terrifying properties in him. He engaged in a sensational boxing match with the then world champion, Jack Johnson, a magnificent black athlete against whose technique Cravan's performance was but amateur's play. He was knocked out all the more swiftly as, in anticipation of the inevitable result, he had arrived in the ring reeling drunk. But this bitter experience left him some money. We saw him often, as well as his brother and charming sister-in-law, Olga Sakharoff, a painter of great talent. Marie Laurençin, now exiled in Barcelona, and formerly one of his most notorious victims, was too intelligent to hold anything against him, so he became one of our little nostalgic, uprooted group. Every day we met at the Café on the Rambla, we dined at each other's lodgings and, for distraction, went in for Spanish cooking. Picabia published the first number of *391*. Then, one day, we learned that Cravan had left for the United States. We met him again in New York in the beginning of 1917. He was in very bad straits, without money, and was trailing along after more fortunate friends, especially the painter, Frost. He seemed worried and restless, for America had also entered the war. He came to see us often in the little apartment in 82nd Street, where chess reigned night and day, where the assaults and calumnies of *391* were planned, where the eccentricities of Marcel Duchamp were admiringly discussed. In March 1917, at the Grand Central Gallery, the American Independents Exhibition took place. Picabia and Duchamp had the idea of having him deliver a lecture there, counting on a repetition of the Paris scandal of 1914. As it happened, things took a rather different turn, one that went beyond all their expectations. Cravan arrived very late, pushing his way through the large crowd of very smart listeners. Obviously drunk, he had difficulty in reaching the lecture platform, his expression and gait showing the decided effects of alcohol. He gesticulated wildly and began to take off his waistcoat. A canvas by the American painter, Sterner, was hanging directly behind him, and the incoherence of his movements made us fear that he would damage it. After having taken off his waistcoat, he began to undo his trousers. The first surprise of the public at his extravagant entrance was soon replaced by murmurs of indignation.

Doubtless the authorities had already been notified, for, at that moment, as he leaned over the table and started hurling one of the most insulting epithets in the English language at his audience, several policemen attacked him suddenly from behind, and handcuffed him with professional skill. He was manhandled, dragged out, and would have been thrown into jail, but for the intervention of Walter Arensberg who bailed him out and took him to his house, while the protesting crowd made a tumultuous exit. If we add that it was a very smart audience, that the most beautiful Fifth Avenue hostesses had been urged to be present — all those who professed interest in painting and had come to be initiated into the new formulae of "futurist" art — it will be seen that the scandal was complete. What a wonderful lecture, said Marcel Duchamp, beaming, when we all met that evening at the home of Arensberg. Cravan, who was still suffering from the effects of his alcoholic orgy, was gloomy and distant, and never spoke of this exploit, which did not make his existence in the United States any easier.

I had the luck to find a position for him as translator in the very correct, puritan family of an old professor of philosophy, who wanted to supervise in person the translation of his works. It meant spending several weeks in the country. I hesitated to speak to Cravan about this situation which would assure him a comfortable existence in exchange for easy work, but which demanded a certain type of conduct I did not dare guarantee. Finally I tackled the problem frankly. "Cravan," I said, "if you will swear to me that you will not carry off the silverware, that you will behave properly with the ladies, that you will not get drunk, etc. etc." He promised everything I asked of him, in such touching, serious terms that I no longer doubted his sincerity, and he was happy as a child at the idea of running around in the woods and living, for a time, far from scandals and alcohol. He kept his promise, perhaps because the ordeal did not last for long, but I give this anecdote as a striking feature of his character, with its multiple sides, of which he himself speaks so movingly in one of his poems.

At that time it became evident that America would have recourse to conscription. The recruiting bureaux for volunteers, which looked like French fair-booths, were stationed in the busiest parts of the city, and did not seem to be very popular, despite the fact that pretty, alluring girls, flanked by a few non-commissioned officers in brand new uniforms, were used as lures. It was their duty to be eloquent through their sex appeal as well as through their patriotism; glory and a kiss were promised to all the poor devils who stopped imprudently to listen. The suggestive haranguing, which was publicly encouraged by prudish America, was to me a daily subject of surprise and amusement; but the lack of enthusiasm on the part of the passers-by made it obvious that more efficacious measures would soon be necessary. Cravan succeeded in escaping again, thanks, perhaps, to the identity papers of his friend Frost, who had died tragically of a tubercular haemorrhage, during a night of orgy and alcohol, in his presence. He went to Canada, was given a lift by passing motorists, who took him for a soldier on furlough, and thus he reached the Far North. A final postal card dated from Newfoundland is the last word I received from him.

Then I returned to France, which means, for the end of this extraordinary story, I have to accept what others have told me. Cravan, it seems, returned to New York, and succeeded in reaching Mexico, accompanied by the British poetess Mina Loy, whom he had met in our circle of friends, and whom he married in Mexico. They had a daughter who is, apparently, the image of her father. In 1918, he was still in Mexico, where he founded a boxing club. He suffered a bad defeat in a fight against a native adversary, which compromised the success of this enterprise. Once more he was without resources and considered the idea of living in other, more favourable countries. Mina Loy had preceded him to Buenos Aires, where he was to join her by sea, on a little yacht that he was equipping little by little for the long journey. Every day he left the town to carry provisions to the yacht, which was anchored farther down the bay. One day he did not come back from his customary visit to the yacht, and since that time nobody has heard of him. It seemed possible for a long time that he might be on some island, or in the prisons of one of the numerous countries at war; and his wife looked for him after the Armistice in every possible place of this kind. But no jail had heard of him, and it has finally become more and more evident that the mystery surrounding the end of this amazing figure will never be cleared up.

■ JACQUES RIGAUT

☐ Some members
of the *Littérature*
group photo-
graphed by Man
Ray in 1922.
Rigaut is seated
centre, bottom row,
flanked by Eluard
and Mick Soupault.
Top row: Serge
Chardoune, Tzara
(pointing a gun at
Rigaut) and
Philippe Soupault.

The weapon aimed at life by the suicide is always right. No rubble nor ruins shall be left standing after the will which burns and destroys everything has passed by. But such an act leaves the strength of whoever has committed it intact. The regret at having been born and the need to die vanishes with the world that they have killed. Alone, absolutely alone and pure, the self-contented thought contemplates and recognises itself. Jacques Rigaut lived under the shadow of this perfect resemblance. Lord Patchogue *attests to this fact.* —PAUL ELUARD.

■ Dandy, drug-addict, gigolo, suicide — Jacques Rigaut was by no means the least intense of all those drawn to Dada in Paris during the opening years of the 1920s. Indeed, Georges Ribemont-Dessaignes in his short *History of Dada* (1931), published two years after Rigaut's death, suggests that his personal example was not without effect in inducing those "cannibalistic" disorders (the term is Tzara's) within the French Dada movement which paved the way for Surrealism:

■ **Introduction:
Jacques Rigaut
by Terry Hale**

Rigaut, a particularly disorganising intelligence, proved to be a Dada among the Dadas, that is, he demoralised whatever came into contact with him, and had not a little to do with the ruin of Dada; in short, he did wonders.

And it is he who was right. *He was irreconcilable with any need for doing, producing, thinking. The unity of opposites, which had been so much discussed, and of those two opposites which epitomise everything, life and death, possessed him entirely. He showed how close he had been to death throughout his life — which ought to be written*

—— by committing suicide in 1929, after having exhausted all the reasons for living a man can offer himself.[28]

As might be imagined from these words, during the course of his short life Rigaut wrote little and published less. The review *Littérature* contains one or two short pieces by him, the last appearing in 1922, but from then on until the time of his death seven years later he maintained an almost unbroken silence. As with Jacques Vaché, who is known to us only through his *Lettres de guerre* and André Breton's reminiscences, Rigaut's influence on the development of the Surrealist movement towards this time could have passed almost without trace. Like Vaché, Rigaut's principle contribution was perhaps his total world-weariness and cynical humour.

His reputation as a writer derives almost entirely from his posthumous works, beginning with *Lord Patchogue*, published in *La Nouvelle Revue Française*[29] shortly after his death, and concluding with the *Agence Générale du Suicide* which did not see the light of day until 1959. His complete extant works, carefully assembled by Martin Kay in 1970, finally constitute a not insubstantial body of texts. In them one finds that continual preoccupation with death for which he was renowned. "Jacques Rigaut sentenced himself to death at about the age of twenty," wrote André Breton in his essay on him in the *Anthologie de l'humour noir*, "and waited impatiently for ten years, ticking off the hours, for exactly the right moment to put an end to his existence. It was, in any case, a fascinating human experience, to which he knew just how to give that peculiar tragi-comic twist which was unique to himself." As Rigaut himself remarks in one of his pieces published in *Littérature*, "Suicide is a vocation." One also finds other recurrent themes too, notably one with mirrors. In *Lord Patchogue*, "that strange fragmentary confession" (as Samuel Putnam once referred to it), the narrator describes himself as "the man on the other side of the mirror" — "the eye that looks at the eye that looks at the eye that looks . . ." Rigaut apparently also experimented with painting or drawing on mirrors.

Independent of his writings, Rigaut's life has given rise to a number of romanticised (and, needless to say, inappropriately moralistic) accounts. Others — including Breton, Eluard, and Desnos — have written more generously. Unfortunately, it is the former which have enjoyed wider currency. They have a common source: Pierre Drieu la Rochelle.

Amazing as it may now seem, such was the climate of uncertainty in the early 1920s that Drieu la Rochelle flirted heavily with the Dada and Surrealist movements for a number of years before his eventual conversion to Fascism. Drieu was a close friend of Rigaut's, though how far removed he was from the spirit which reigned at *Littérature* may be clearly seen from the guarded nature of his replies when called as a witness during the Barrès trial.

In 1921, under the auspices of Dada but at the initiative of Aragon and Breton, it was decided to put Maurice Barrès, the nationalist writer, on trial. The event was the last public scandal of Paris Dada, the appearance of Benjamin Péret as a witness in a German uniform while being referred to as "The Unknown Soldier," causing universal press hysteria. Breton presided, Ribemont-Dessaignes acted for the prosecution, Aragon and Soupault defended. Rigaut's testimony was very different to the sort of unsatisfactory replies given by Drieu:

Q. Do you find Barrès antipathetic or sympathetic?
A. I don't know, but I feel respect for him.

Drieu la Rochelle came to hate anything in which he detected signs of bourgeois decadence. Dada and Surrealism were, for him, temporary outlets for his frustration against a society which he considered had grown corrupt. What he really wanted was not a Surrealist Revolution but a return to a moral order. Despite being at one time a close personal friend, a less suitable biographer — even if only in the context of fictional writings — for Rigaut is hard to imagine. Though Drieu obviously loved his friend dearly, his writings about him are thinly disguised political fables of what he perceived as degeneration.

Drieu first wrote about Rigaut in 1924: an unpleasant short story entitled *La Valise Vide* [The Empty Suitcase]. After his suicide, he deeply regretted having penned this piece, confiding in his diary: "I killed you Rigaut. I could have warmed you against my breast."[30] This did not prevent him from writing a novel concerning the last few days of Rigaut's life (*Le Feu Follet*, 1931; tr. *Will o' the Wisp*, Calder & Boyars, 1966) which was filmed in 1966 by Louis Malle. In Drieu's novel, Rigaut (who is called Alain) is portrayed as a victim of the directionless hedonism of the 1920s, one whose existential crisis could simply have been resolved by a steady job, a more disciplined society. No doubt Drieu's bourgeois readership found something reassuring in these trite assumptions . . .

Jacques Rigaut was born in 1898, the son of the buyer for a department store (according to Desnos). His impoverished dandyism perhaps resembles in many respects that of certain nineteenth-century writers such as Charles Lassailly. Indeed David Gascoyne, in *Atlas Anthology III*, compared Rigaut's *persona* Lord Patchogue with Huysmans' Des Esseintes and Hugo von Hofmaansthal's Lord Chandos. After the First World War he read law while working as the secretary of the French academic painter, Jacques-Émile Blanche (whose appreciation of his secretary follows Rigaut's texts here). In 1924, shortly after the demise of Paris Dada, he met an extremely rich young American divorcee whom he followed to New York and married in 1926. The marriage was not a success. By the following year they had already separated, Rigaut remaining in New York, often desperately short of money and increasingly addicted to alcohol and heroin. In 1928, he suddenly decided to return to France, where he attempted a number of detoxification cures without success. Finally, on the morning of 6 November 1929, he returned to the clinic where he was staying at Châtenay-Malabry and — "after paying minute attention to his toilette, and carrying out all the necessary external adjustments demanded of such a departure" (André Breton) — calmly shot himself through the heart. He had used a ruler in order to be sure that he would not miss his heart, and a pillow in order to muffle the sound of the report. He had even taken care to put a rubber sheet under his body so as to avoid staining the bed.[31]

"Try, if you can" wrote Jacques Rigaut, "to arrest a man who travels with suicide in his buttonhole." (*Pensées*, 79)

□ Rigaut, Tzara,
Breton, early 1920s.

■ A state-licenced company.
Capital: 5,000,000 Francs.
Principal Paris Office: 73, Boulevard Montparnasse.
Branches in Lyons, Bordeaux, Marseilles, Dublin, Monte Carlo, San Francisco.

■ **The General Suicide Agency**

Due to technological advances, the GSA is pleased to announce to its clients that it can now GUARANTEE THEM AN INSTANTANEOUS DEATH. This service cannot fail to be of interest to those who have previously been deterred from committing suicide for fear of "making a mess of it." It is with a view to the elimination of the unhappy and the desperate, who always represent a dangerous source of contagion in society, that the Minister of the Interior has graciously consented to act as our honorary president.

Amongst other benefits, the GSA at last offers a reputable method of passing away, death being the least excusable of moral failings. That is why we have organised an Express Burial service: meal, viewing by friends and relations, photographs (or death masks if preferred), distribution of effects, suicide, placing in coffin, religious ceremony (optional), transport of the body to the cemetery. The GSA pledges itself to carry out the last wishes of its esteemed clients.

N.B. — In the event of the establishment not being close to a main thoroughfare, the corpse will be conveyed to the morgue in order to ensure the peace of mind of those families who so desire it.

PRICE LIST

Electrocution	200 fr.
Revolver	100 fr.
Poison	100 fr.
Drowning	50 fr.

Perfumed Death (inclusive of luxury tax) 500 fr.
Hanging. The suicide of the poor. (The rope is charged at 20 fr. per metre, plus 5 fr. for every additional 10 cm.) 5 fr.

Ask for our special Express Burials catalogue.
All enquiries to:
Monsieur J. Rigaut, Principal Director,
73, Boulevard Montparnasse, Paris, 75006.
Correspondence requesting a wish to attend a suicide shall be ignored.

■ **1.** Here is Lord Patchogue. You know how to recognise him. If not him, you will know how to recognise another more surely, no doubt, than he would be able to do so himself. Despite his dark complexion, his profile, his bearing, his distinguished appearance, the nobility of his features, the self-control of his expression, there is a certain weakness which seems out of place, a vulnerable quality.

Is it to help you or is it to help himself that Lord Patchogue tries so hard: his clothes are always alike — though not the same, for he is careful of his appearance — identical, the same cut, the same colour, as if he were afraid that a new outfit would change him.

■ **2.** Touch my forehead. Good! Now look at your fingers, they are stained with my blood.

It is the conventions of the language which makes me say my *forehead* and my *blood*. If I doubt *my* existence, it is not existence which I wish to contest, only that it should be mine. The usage of possessive pronouns is forbidden me. Let me explain.

The name by which I am known is Lord Patchogue (there is no need to tell you that Patchogue, the town from which my name is taken, has never existed). I have a distinguished appearance . . . I also clearly remember that my face reminds me of yours.

Look at me, my face; do you not detect a close resemblance, it is hardly surprising — I look like everybody. You will learn why later. Say it aloud then, or are you afraid now: that I resemble you, that I am your living image. You are standing before a mirror. Let me explain.

■ **Lord Patchogue I. Before**

My story should begin with mirrors, or else by the impossible possessive — I wonder. Lord Patchogue, as I said before, is my name. But although this is the name to which I habitually answer, to tell the truth I am not totally convinced that it is mine.

■ **3.** The room, its four walls, is unbearable. I have to get out. I no longer know which streets to avoid, those one already knows because one already knows them, those one doesn't know for the same reason or for another. I suspect the soles of my shoes were not made for these pavements, my legs for these trousers, nor my patience for this waiting. Great feats, low deeds, acrobatics, records, the greatest difficulty of all is to breathe.

■ **4.** Cowardice — all of Lord Patchogue's dignity is contained in this word.

How much can one put up with?

The beginning is honest: every proposition being unacceptable, every posture undesirable; all that is left is a tense, indolent refusal as gestures, desires and thoughts move ever nearer the shell.

What happens next is less so: whatever he does and whatever he does not do, Lord Patchogue calls it his cowardice; one can no longer fool oneself.

■ **5.** This regime of the surrounding error, these enthusiasms like drownings, this order like my father's alphabet, what assistance can they lend the observer's assurance?

Two legs are insufficient to guarantee Lord Patchogue's balance, and this balance, were one to offer him the formula, how could he not reject it as *an even more mortal* danger?

■ 6. And even as I affirm, still I interrogate.

■ 7. For the credulous, there is no difference between winning and losing. If there is nothing to be gained, what can there be to lose? That is the route the devil has taken, we have already picked up his tracks, a grey pointed wing at the hour of grace. Lord Patchogue becomes increasingly drunk on the worst possible vanity: losing. He is punctual on every occasion, it is his only appointment. To waste away, become emaciated — melt away — what intoxication. The sign: a national song, the password of the initiates of the heart. Month by month, if not day by day, finds him less adept at handling all those things which serve to be discovered, to move, to bewilder; his concentration becomes rusted. Those perspectives, those forbidden panoramas, does the contemplation of his shell recompense him for them? He smiles: "I will soon hold the key in a single word."

He has sought refuge in his cowardice, to each his own dignity.

■ 8. Lord Patchogue is not afraid to speak provided that the subject is himself and there is only one interlocutor. Concerning himself, that is an act of modesty on his part, even if it hardly suits you. A single interlocutor is not to be feared, even the Pope can be persuaded to become a counterfeit in a face to face interview. More than one is a crowd, an understanding smile between you and Lord Patchogue is disarmed, panic-stricken: if there are only a few of you — and two suffices — then one can put the world to rights and put it back again. There is only one madman in the mental asylum and he is clearly the governor.

■ **9.** NOTE: In a similar case, though in rather different circumstances, Lord Patchogue spent six months exclusively preoccupied by a creature who could not have the least possible interest for him. Love, comfort, vanity, money: she could offer him none of these. What was more, he considered their relationship intensely boring. This did not prevent him from having eyes only for her during the six months their union lasted; as for his friends, he had ceased to see them except for one or two with whom he could discuss the matter. His proclivity for monsters which was undoubtedly at the bottom of this episode cannot by itself explain the persistence of such disinterested fascination. In any event, he later lost all interest and would be incapable of rationalising it.

Which did not prevent him from finding another reason to justify his interest.

■ **10.** The interest alone was valid, at least, *who can find his path without recourse to the senses.* The five illegitimate senses. By "interest" should be understood the stake, the promise of some comfort, a pleasure, a discovery.

■ **11.** The greater my disinterest, the more authentic is my interest.

■ **12.** I lay no special claims to indifference based on non-participation. I go red like anyone else. Red with heat, white with cold, I will slap you with my hand if you stand on my feet. You will have no trouble catching me out in all sorts of emotional and physical transgressions.

But do not become involved in my adventures.

■ **13.** I cross my legs, I knock against the muscle behind my knee-cap, my leg jerks in the air. Where do I come in? You will say that it was me who moved.

How do you see Lord Patchogue in all this? What was his portion, what was his role?

■ **14.** Lord Patchogue is like everyone else, of course. He would be the first to admit it, not that it means very much. All around him, everybody (it goes without saying) would be too idle ever to suspect it, did he not proclaim as much himself and in such a vehement manner as alone to be sufficient to arouse suspicions.

Lord Patchogue answers to his name, does not confuse it with that of another, no matter how strong the temptation. In the meanwhile, your ten fingers do not belong to him and that point between his two eyes is not in the middle of your face. You rise to your feet, is it really you, perhaps it is he, it is not impossible.

■ **15.** He has been seen exercising various trades, wearing different hats, he has kept neither one nor the other. Lord Patchogue has proved no more faithful to an ambition, a desire or a pledge. It takes two to succeed; ambition, desire, pledge and someone else as well. Since Lord Patchogue doubts his own existence, all he needs to do is claim what he has borrowed.

■ **16.** Lord Patchogue dashes to the mirror to assure himself that he is still there, not really he himself, but his nose, the nose that he saw only a few minutes ago. It is not so much his existence he doubts as that of each of his attributes, and if not of their existence then of their legitimacy.

■ **17.** When he makes love, he shouts his own name, as if to strike his adversary, like a second means of scattering his semen.

■ **18.** His laziness has won out against his affectation. A few years ago you would have been able to catch out Lord Patchogue making defensive errors against taste, preferences, choice. Errors of taste.

■ **19.** He probably desires all that a man possesses, or at least enough to let him forget that he owns nothing. Just to want would suffice. But Lord Patchogue does not even want to want.

■ He is sitting in front of a table occupied with a game of patience. Does he exist? He is between two cards, then he is the movement of one card towards another; it is into that moment that the universe is reduced — nine of hearts on ten of clubs. That's it. Lord Patchogue raises his head, the universe revives. The supernumeraries in another corner of the room are making a row.

In an enormous mirror on the wall opposite, Lord Patchogue catches a glimpse of his reflection: "I know you. I do not mistake you for an ostrich, nor for a street-lamp, nor for a friend of Charles. You are the reflection of Lord Patchogue, that is if you are not Lord Patchogue himself. Ah! Which of the two of us moved first? Who is imitating the other?"

Lord Patchogue stands up. He studies his full-length portrait in the mirror. Five senses are not sufficient for his chance companions; once more they shall miss the show; they are no more ready to perceive the presence of a mystery than they think of death.

Lord Patchogue and his reflection slowly advance towards each other. They consider each other in silence, they come to a halt, they bow.

A great dizziness seizes hold of Lord Patchogue. It was brief, easily done, and magical: forehead first, he suddenly springs forwards. He strikes the glass, which shatters, but there he is on the other side.

Everyone had stood up.

The marvellous is not rare, incredulity is stronger than miracles. Miracles have difficulty in recruiting witnesses amongst the small number of people prepared to subscribe to the supernatural. Lord Patchogue was the first to be unsure that he had crossed the threshold. None of those who crowded around him noticed the astonishing disappearance of their friend. They surrounded him as if he was still

■ **II. Episode In The Mirror At Oyster Bay**

there, they recognised him, they can hear his voice.

A certain malaise arose however. Why had not Lord Patchogue hurt himself more seriously? The single delicate diagonal cut on his forehead is not enough; one cannot traverse a mirror with impunity, it is not possible; everyone would have felt more reassured if they had been able to count numerous bloody injuries. Only one person, the same one who will officiate for the rest of the evening, has suspected the fatal nature of the thin red gash which disfigures Lord Patchogue's forehead.

News of a miracle does not spread so easily; it knows what has to be done and assists itself with extraordinary manifestations. Oblivious as they were, Lord Patchogue's companions, even if they can smile about it today, did not fail to behave in a singular manner.

Why did Simon pick up the debris of the broken mirror and place it splinter by splinter on a large tea tray? Why, when he had done this, did he carry this, his work, with a gravity which already marked the face of Lord Patchogue more visibly than his own, this little pile of crystals and fragments into the bedroom of Muriel, who was already laid out barefoot, and place it on the bed?

Why did Muriel begin to trample on the splinters of glass as if dancing, as if making a sacrifice, and, above all, despite the violence of her actions, why did her feet remain unscathed by any cuts?

Only Lord Patchogue's forehead bled imperceptibly.

Douglas went out in order to vomit. The others prayed.

The next day, two workmen came to replace the mirror. By the time they had finished, Lord Patchogue had disappeared.

■ **1.** The reverse is just as good as the right side: it is necessary to wait there.

■ **2.** First customer —

How to stop him? I know everything he is going to tell me. That's enough. I can predict his every move. Do not open your mouth, simpleton. I know what you will have to say tomorrow, I know you from the front, behind, north, south, hot, cold; that's enough.

Do not open your mouth, my friend. To whom are you speaking, you are drunk, my ears are your ears, your tongue is my own, you are alone, madmen make me afraid.

"My friend's sweethearts . . ."

". . . are my sweethearts." I can complete all your sentences.

■ **3.** When tiredness overcomes Lord Patchogue at his observation post, when he became certain that he would not discover anything except a confirmation, he turns round, a mirror is behind him and Lord Patchogue sees himself again. They both say to one another in fearful tones which only increase as they contemplate themselves: "I am a man trying not to die." And Lord Patchogue launches himself through the mirror a second time. A crash of splintering glass. Lord Patchogue stands before another mirror, facing Lord Patchogue. On his forehead, the cut is bleeding once again. Lord Patchogue repeats: "I am a man trying not to die." And when he passes through the third mirror amidst a noise which is now familiar, he knows that he will meet Lord Patchogue whose forehead will be bleeding more heavily in the fourth mirror and who will tell him: "I am a man trying not to die." This is what happens. Now he knows, all he can do is to break the glass; the eye that looks at the eye that looks at the eye that looks . . .

The man trying not to die has propelled himself; he walks automatically, without curiosity, without 'expectation,' because he cannot do otherwise, with each step another mirror shatters; he walks surrounded by the crash which soothes the ear of the condemned man; before each mirror he chants: "... the eye — that looks at the eye — that looks at the eye — that looks at the eye — that looks . . . " Lord Patchogue stops. The floor is nothing but a broken mirror, not just the floor but also the walls and ceiling. Pretty landscape, the walls and ceiling lodge in the debris of mirrors as best they can.

■ **4.** Lord Patchogue has a plan. So much the worse for the first person to happen by. Wait. At last the sound of footsteps approaching the caged hunter. Someone is in the room, someone who is still out of sight of the mirror. Will the mirror's call really be in vain? No, whoever it is approaches. Alas, it's a woman.

"Cheated! Clear off, sugar! Next please!"

She preens herself professionally. Disarmed, Lord Patchogue passively returns to her what she desires. What love, what lovers, what what. The young woman is more than self-satisfied, she runs her hands over her breasts. Lord Patchogue reflects her movements with docility, all it takes to recall him to himself is the contact of the two young unknown globes under his fingers. Over her blouse, his fingers cautiously linger on a woman's breast as she breathes in, he feels her swell, he receives her warmth.

In order to adjust a stocking, she reveals a leg with the indifferent precision of someone who knows that nobody can possibly be watching. Lord Patchogue obedient to the unstated wish offers her a leg for the sake of love.

He can hardly believe his eyes, and over her blouse his fingers cautiously linger on a woman's chest, his own, at his own body temperature, rising as she breathes. But would the transformation stop with the breasts or . . . And a comic inquietude seizes hold of Lord Patchogue, so compelling is the superstition of male virility that instead of hoping for the acquisition of a new sex, Lord Patchogue with a furtive but revealing gesture checks to assure himself that he is still a man. As he prepares himself to inhale, there is a scream from in front of him. Because unfortunately the young girl, now passive in her turn, can do no more than imitate the movement of Lord Patchogue. And what a discovery: attributes which only marriage should reveal to her. The victim might well run off, but towards what dreams!

■ **5.** There is no way out on this side, any progress is impossible, the ladder of eyes stretches to infinity. In front of him, it would be enough to traverse the mirror in the opposite direction, taking every conceivable precaution of course, a blow with the heel to begin with would suffice; but would that not be to return to his hat size and wouldn't the nine letters of his name coil themselves around his neck like the chains on which identity medallions hang; undesirable. The walls, there were still the walls; Lord Patchogue approaches, touches them with his finger, pushes; but even the mirrors offer less resistance to his efforts.

Young unknown, your hair is out of place; to tidy it, thoughtless little fly, you approach the mirror. Watch out, Lord Patchogue has a plan. But what's the use, the breeze which has mussed your hair must have received precise instructions from the proper authority. The imprudent one stops; on the other side Lord Patchogue steadies himself; like an athlete flexing his muscles before the race, assuring himself of their suppleness, he raises both his hands on a level with his tie, and the victim does likewise. Everything is working. He brings his hand to his tie and adjusts it slightly, then he flicks back his hair once or twice, just like the other. Lord Patchogue is sure of him now. He slowly turns his head so that the mirror is no longer in the victim's field of vision and with unexpected vigour throws himself to one side, against, into, through the wall. When the subject turns his head again, all he can do is remark that he has taken the place of Lord Patchogue. The right side is just as good as the reverse.

■ **6.** Alternate dialogue and monologue between the visitors and Lord Patchogue:

"It is I who am looking at you and it is you that you see, you're incorrigible."

■ **7.** My ten fingers are not your fingers and this point between my eyes is not in the middle of your face. I rarely feel pain when someone strikes you, any more than you do for me.

■ **8.** Sign your name, naturally, at the bottom of this mirror, etch it, provided that it contains neither a 'p', nor a 't', nor a 'c', nor an 'h', nor an 'o', nor a 'g', nor an 'a', nor a 'u', nor an 'e'.

■ **9.** Just like a photographer: "Smile, and I'll do the rest."

■ **10.** Don't forget that I cannot see myself, that my role is limited to being the one who looks in the mirror while at the same time I remain Patchogue as before. I have never felt so natural.

(Nothing has changed.)

■ **1.** The secret: life begins with anomaly, with an abnormal function. The wheel which turns, etc. The legs. . .

■ **IV. The Escape**

■ **2.** Once and for all, I am not telling you the story of my life, only a story which I remember. Nothing happens, or at least nothing ever happened.

■ **3.** In all these things which should give rise to dread in me, should affect me, I feel nothing, I do not see myself, I am not there. There are, no doubt, those people who are able to adapt to the impossible, liberty, impossible liberty, provided that there are no more questions.

■ **4.** Lord Patchogue walks a body which demonstrates the same resistance, a body that you will recognise. The voice is the same, that which you have already heard, it has the same sharply-defined features, only that vulnerable quality has disappeared, the weakness through which the mortal air of your own breath may pass. The mechanism is the same and the eye has not ceased to transmit to the eye on the next rung his observation, which incessantly proceeds from eye to eye. [...]

■ **V. (Fragment)**   ■ Note:

For those who appreciate the marvellous, this is how Lord Patchogue got his name. Travelling around Long Island with some friends in a car, near New York, Mrs Muriel Draper — someone of whom I could say far too much, but above all a friend of mine — and myself found our attention drawn along those endless roads devoid of signposts by one which indicated the way to the town of Patchogue at almost every cross-roads. We drove along these roads for three days obsessed by this signpost (just like the one reading "Vichy 794 km" which one sees on every road in France) without ever managing to reach the aforesaid town. Without us realising, the word took on the meaning of something which does not exist in our conversation. A couple of weeks later we learned from the newspapers that some artful man had managed to persuade half the population of Patchogue that the end of the world would occur on a particular day and had succeeded in buying cheap a vast expanse of land.

The following summer, I found myself in Italy on a friend's small boat in the Gulf of Naples. We stopped off at the Albergo della Luna at Amalfi. In this hotel I came across notepaper [...]. Under the heading Albergo della Luna there was a large reproduction of the patio of the inn, and in the middle of this design an inset portrait of the face of Ibsen with a caption surrounding it to the effect that Henrik Ibsen had etc., etc. I thought that this notepaper would amuse my friends and decided to send a specimen to Mrs Muriel Draper. I also had at this time amongst other conceits that of writing my letters in the form of the contents page of a book: something which catered for both my laziness and my desire not to miss the opportunity of delivering to the recipient of the letter at our next meeting an account of such incidents as the title of each chapter would serve to recall.

for André Breton

■ A Brilliant Individual

■ It is possible to conceive of a mobile structure moving at such a speed that following the line of the Equator in the opposite direction to the planet's rotation it circles the earth before the latter has had time to displace itself more than fractionally. With a few equations and a good reputation, it is as easy to represent time as a spiral as it is to describe real time or the passage of time, and a mobile stucture starting its trajectory at midday from any given point would travel through 6.00 a.m., midnight, 6.00 p.m. before arriving at noon the previous day — and so on.

A divorced engineer constructed a machine in the form of a giant egg which, by means of the different temperatures that can be obtained by the use of electricity while leaving that of the cabin inside unaffected, was capable of going back in time. One cause for concern remained: it was feared that the traveller might grow younger during the course of his expedition, that one might even find nothing more than a baby at the first stopover, or, if the journey was a prolonged one, the traveller's father amd mother, perhaps his entire lineage, squashed together inside the machine.

A sentimental young man — by the name of Skullhead — was eager to take advantage of this invention in order to sort out his life. His main preoccupation was to locate a mistress whom he had lost seven years before and recommence their liaison as many times as necessary to establish a mutual love between them.

Departure of Skullhead; arrival of Skullhead. He dashes into his mistress's apartment. "Me first!" he exclaims on finding himself confronted by a twenty-year-old Skullhead stretched out in her bed. "I hadn't quite calculated the extent of the past. I suppose that if I carried off the Skullhead here before me in the egg, at the rate of one stopover per year I could encounter myself at every stage of my life and end up faced with some twenty plus versions of myself of various sizes all in the same room."

Rivalry between Skullhead and Skullhead[1]. Skullhead, having the advantage of knowing what was going to happen, supplants Skullhead[1]. Skullhead[1], in despair, threatens to commit suicide. Skullhead, by now frightened that this suicide might entail his own death, cedes his place to Skullhead[1] and clambers back into his machine.

Feeling the need to stretch his legs, Skullhead goes back twenty-three years in the past in the same country. Various incests are consummated. Skullhead becomes of the opinion that he is his own father.

"Napoleon, Hannibal, the Pyramids! Humph! Back to the Flood!" exclaims Skullhead, pressing a device designed to register his heart-beats against his chest in order to calculate his age. Skullhead is once more on his way in search of Genesis.

Uncertain of meeting God and powerless to modify a past from which he himself was issued, Skullhead concentrates on creating new versions which are just sufficiently different enough to perplex those of his contemporaries who might subsequently venture back into the past only to find nothing there any longer that corresponded with their historical expectations.

Towards the end of the reign of the Emperor Augustus, Skullhead, after roaming the province of Judea for six months, stumbles across a child who is Jesus of Nazareth asleep under an olive tree: he injects potassium cyanide into the child's veins.

A few years further back, he remained on the lookout for a little Egyptian girl during his walks. One day, coming across her alone, he threw himself upon her and mutilated her nose with his gas pliers. The name of this girl was Cleopatra.

Stopping off in South America, Skullhead explained the use of steam and electricity to the Red Indians. He became worshipped as a god, and every month fifty virgins and fifty young boys were handed over to satisfy his pleasure.

Throughout the five continents, Skullhead preached the doctrine of obligatory suicide at the age of twenty.

He presented to Homer a copy of Tristan Tzara's *Deuxième aventure céleste de Monsieur Antipyrine*.

Skullhead achieved renown for his prophecies under the various pseudonyms of Ezekiel, Jeremiah and Isiah.

Skullhead was not immune to human passions. He fell in love with a Hindu courtesan. Unable to bear the climate, Skullhead missed out the summers and devoted only the winter months to her. Becoming so attached to this logical premise, he no longer made love to her one time after another but, rather, one time before another, until she died as a result at the age of seven.

His food supplies on board having run out, Skullhead was frequently obliged to stop. He spent several months playing at god so that he could build up his stock of provisions. A white beard began to hide his chest. Skullhead finally died of old age in the egg which is still circling the earth.

■ One has made such a lot of love only because it is of greater utility than other things. The more necessary money becomes the more demanding, the more wonderful and agreeable it becomes, like love. One could just as easily argue the reverse. My poverty is easier to bear if I remember that there are people who are rich. Other people's money helps me live, but not quite as you might imagine. Every Rolls-Royce that I chance upon prolongs my life by a quarter of an hour. Rather than doff their hats to the undertaker's hearse, people would be better advised to salute Rolls-Royces.

Thought is a task for the poor, a wretched revenge. When I am alone, I do not think. I think only when forced; the compulsion: the minor examination to prepare for, paternal obligations, the trade to which I must submit myself, all salaried work leads me to thought, that is to say to making up my mind to kill myself, which is the same thing. There are few different ways of thinking; to think is to reflect on death and arrive at a decision. — Otherwise, I sleep. Praise be to sleep! not only the magnificent mystery of each night, but also to unpredictable torpor. My companions of sleep, it is in your company that I imagine a satisfactory existence. We will sleep behind the throb of motors, we will sleep with skis on our feet, we will sleep before the smoking cities, in the blood of ports, above the desert, we will sleep on the stomachs of our women, we will sleep in the pursuit of knowledge, armed with our Crookes's tube and syllogisms — the seekers of sleep.

As I roar past in my nHP, let the poets beware and not linger in the safety of the avenues lest I become the subject of some small item in

■ **Story of a Poor Young Man**

the newspapers! This thinker turns his nose up at dollars, but of course! he holds reality in the palm of his hand, but of course! Meanwhile, there he is, on the pavement, in the queue, waiting for a place on the bus, and as I pass close by him in my car I smile with pleasure as I splash him with mud, along with a few other under-nourished specimens, and he mutters: "Idiot!"

"Idiot yourself! I'm asleep." You, in your office, angry or bored, you think of death, wretched victim! You have a good understanding of love! All the same, one permits oneself a certain indulgence for these women when one recalls what rivals they have produced for their poet-lovers! Just you wait until I am the richest man in the world and see who will be responsible for ignoble urges at my place! Sssh! The thinkers are grooming my cars! Now who is laughing? Do you not appreciate the advantage of all my millions; that they are a state of grace? I shall have the first exact balance at last; I know the price of things; every pleasure will be priced. Consult the menu. *Love for sale.* That should insure me against the passions! I can do without people's consent, and I shall rub my hands if their agreement is replaced by sacrifice and against-my-wills.

A well-wisher, a man twenty years older than myself, has offered me a means of subsistence so that I need not give up the speculative life for which I have demonstrated such a natural disposition — he must be joking! — to classify all the index-cards in a library and to edit an anthology of the lofty thoughts of some great general or monarch. Badly shaken, all I could think to say to this worthy man was that I would prefer to be dragged before the Assize Courts rather than sink so low as to accept such employment. Praise God! There is still the Stock Exchange, entry to which is open even to the non-Jewish. And there is no shortage of other ways of stealing. It is a shameful business earning money. How can a doctor avoid blushing when a patient places a bank-note on his desk As soon as a gentleman places himself in the position of accepting money from someone, he might as well wait until he is asked to lower his trousers. If one does not render a service freely, why render it at all? Clearly, I have to turn to crime from a sense of delicacy.

The charming V——— has just married a wealthy young boy; she is in love with him. It is not his money that she loves, she loves him because he is rich. Wealth is a moral quality. The eyes, the furs, health, the legs, the hands, the Packard 12, the skin, the bearing, the reputation, the pearls, the prejudices, the perfume, the teeth, the ardour, the dresses straight from the great couturier, the breasts, the voice, the house on the Avenue du Bois, the imagination, the place in society, the ankles, the make-up, the tenderness, the prowess at tennis, the smile, the hair, the silk, I make no distinction between these things, and none of them is any less seductive than another.

One has never lived on anything but hope, and the tiny blue cubes which circulate — in various sizes — from one player to another across the green baize of the baccarat hall are something quite different from Juliette's balcony. A big win. Around the table expressions change in slow motion, smiles break out unwillingly and paralyse trembling fingers. I understood what respect was when early one morning I saw the woman who was carrying several years of insolence in her handbag leave the casino and meet on the road outside the women who fish for shrimps returning from the sea, damp, laden down with nets and barefoot.

Young man, mediocre, poor, 21 years old, clean hands, seeks wife, 24 cylinders, healthy, sex maniac or fluent in Anamese. Write Jacques Rigault,[32] 73 Boulevard du Montparnasse, Paris, 75006.

■ Jacques Rigaut

■ I shall be serious, as serious as pleasure. People don't know what they're talking about. There are no reasons for living, but there are no reasons for dying either. The only means which are granted us to express our contempt for life is to accept it. Life is not worth the trouble of departing from it. One may, as an act of kindness, refuse it on behalf of another, but for oneself? Despair, indifference, betrayals, faithfulness, solitude, family, liberty, weariness, money, poverty, love, the absence of love, syphilis, health, sleep, insomnia, desire, impotence, banality, art, honesty, mediocrity, intelligence — none of these things are worth a damn. We understand them only too well to pay them any notice; just sufficient to furnish a few accidental suicides. (Physical pain, no doubt, is another matter. Personally, I am perfectly well. Too bad for those who have a pain in the liver. I've never had much time for victims, though I can sympathise with people who think they would be unable to bear dying of cancer.) Besides, isn't it this revolver, this revolver with which we shall do away with ourselves tonight if we have half a mind that liberates us and removes any possibility of suffering. Anger and despair, on the other hand, have never been anything more than fresh reasons for clinging to life. It's very handy, suicide: so handy that I can't stop thinking about it: I haven't killed myself yet. There is still one lingering regret: one doesn't wish to depart before compromising oneself: it would be good to take with us the Virgin Mary, love or the Republic.

Suicide should be a vocation. The blood circulates and demands a justification for its interminable journey. There is an impatience in fingers which squeeze only the hollow of the hand. There is an itch for an activity which rebounds on itself if the wretch has neglected to learn how to choose an objective. Abstract desires. Impossible desires. This is where the line is drawn between suffering which has a name and a goal and that which is anonymous and self-induced. It is like a pubertal stage of the mind, just as described in novels (naturally, I was corrupted too young to have experienced the crisis at the moment a paunch starts to form), though one gets over it in ways other than by committing suicide.

There's not much I have taken very seriously; as a child I stuck my tongue out at the poor women who accosted my mother in the street and asked for alms and on the sly I pinched their brats who were weeping with cold; when my dying father wanted to confide his last wishes to me and called me to his bedside, I grabbed hold of the maid and sang: *Your parents we must outwit, — You'll see why you're my favourite. . .* Wherever there was a chance to betray a friend's confidence, I think I never missed it. But there is little merit in jeering at kindness or ridiculing charity, and the surest way of raising a laugh is to deprive people of their little lives — without motive, just for fun. Children do not deceive themselves and know how to savour the pleasure of throwing an ant hill into panic or squashing two flies surprised in the act of copulating. During the war I threw a grenade into a dug-out where two friends were getting ready to go on leave. How I laughed when I saw my mistress's face when, as she waited for a kiss, I slugged her with my fist so hard her body landed a yard away; and what a sight, all those people struggling to leave the Gaumont Palace after I had set fire to it! Tonight, though, you have nothing to fear, I am in a serious mood. — There is obviously not a word of truth in these stories and I was the best behaved little boy in Paris, but I have so often delighted in imagining that I had accomplished or that I would accomplish such honourable exploits that it isn't exactly a lie either. Anyway, I scoffed at quite a lot! One thing I never managed to bring myself to scoff at though: pleasure. If I were still capable of shame or self-respect, you can well imagine that I would not choose to impart such a painful confidence. Another day I will explain to you why I never lie: one has nothing to hide from one's servants. But to return to pleasure, which promises to overtake you and, with two little notes of music, win you over to the idea of skin and many other things besides. As long as I cannot overcome my taste for pleasure, I well know that I shall be susceptible to the intoxication of suicide.

The first time that I killed myself it was to annoy my mistress. That virtuous creature brusquely refused to sleep with me, saying that she was overcome by remorse for cheating on her number one lover. I don't really know if I loved her, I suspect that a fortnight away from her would have singularly diminished the need I had for her: but her refusal exasperated me. How to get back at her? Have I said that she retained a deep and lasting affection for me? I killed myself to annoy my mistress. My suicide may be forgiven taking into consideration my extreme youth at the time.

The second time I killed myself it was from laziness. Poor, and having an anticipatory horror of work, one day I killed myself as I had lived — without conviction. They do not hold this death against me when they see how I am flourishing today.

The third time — I will spare you the details of my other suicides, provided that you agree to listen to this one: I had just gone to bed after an evening on which my boredom had been no more overwhelming than any other night. I took the decision and, at the same time, I clearly remember that I articulated the sole reason. Then, drat! I got up to go and look for the only weapon in the house, a little revolver that one of my grandfathers had bought and which was loaded with bullets from the same epoch. (You will see in a moment why I stress this detail.) Lying down naked on my bed, I was naked in the room. It was cold. I hurriedly buried myself under the blankets. I cocked the hammer, I could feel the cold of the steel in my mouth. At that moment I could probably feel my heart beating, just as I could feel it beating as I listened to the whistle of a shell before it exploded, as if in the presence of something irrevocable but still unconsummated. I pressed the trigger, the hammer clicked, but the shot didn't fire. I then laid the weapon on a small table, probably laughing a little nervously. Ten minutes later, I was asleep. I think that I just made a rather important remark. What was it again? But of course! It goes without saying that I did not for an instant consider firing a second shot. The important thing was not whether I died or not but that I had taken the decision to die.

A man who has been spared by dullness and boredom may perhaps find in suicide the accomplishment of a most selfless gesture, provided that he is not curious about death! I have absolutely no idea when and how I could have thought like this, which hardly troubles me in any case. But, all the same, it is the most absurd of acts, and a fantasy at the moment it shatters, and a lack of constraint beyond sleep, and the purest of compromises.

■ **Witness:** *A Young Man of the Century* by Jacques-Émile Blanche

□ *Self-portrait* by Jacques-Émile Blanche (1861-1942), one of the most fashionable portrait painters of his day

■ [*Blanche's essay begins by quoting the entire penultimate paragraph of the previous text.*] In the interval between this contemplated suicide and the real one, there was a period of ten years, more or less, during which I cared for Jacques Rigaut, as for one of those wayward sons for whom a mother, a father, his sisters are every day led to fear the worst. Having learned of the mysterious suicide of one of his forebears, he believed that he was the victim of a fatal heredity; his days were numbered, so why not taste all the *nourritures terrestres*, why not find an alibi in the *paradis artificiels* . . . ? He took little trouble to hide from us his excesses of folly. The catastrophe struck me as being inevitable from the day I made the acquaintance of this charming personality at the house of a friend who, almost jestingly, suggested him as a secretary. Rigaut was glad to have it known that he was "employed by a writer," in order to ward off the threats of a very bourgeois family, bent upon "putting into business" an idle and spendthrift youngster whose upkeep was ruinous.

Upon coming back from the trenches, he still had to put in a few months of barracks-duty. Very proud of his apprentice-warrior's lack of sensitivity, this hypersensitive young man boasted of having had no feeling whatsoever as he saw his dearest comrade drop at his side. A haughty attitude and, what is more, one quite in fashion at the time in Dada circles. My first glimpse of him was in the shadows of a study, where M. X——, weird thaumaturge, a professor of rhetoric by profession, was evoking for a disconsolate brother the spirit of an officer who had fallen at Verdun. The hero was to appear seated upon a chair that was waiting for him. My horror at this occultism would have led me to flee the macabre scene, had it not been for Jacques, who was looking on with some credulity, I fear. As we left, he laughed "a bit nervously," as he usually did. It was his little way of warding off a sneer when overcome with emotion.

"Sir," he said to me, "I may impress you as being too *gigolo*, but I beg you to give me a trial anyway."

He had begun as secretary to Abel Hermant. Their daily relations had not been altogether smooth. Jacques Rigaut, being on the look-out for a job that would not require his getting up so early in the morning, and which would assure him of more leisure, had fallen back on me. Happy telepathy — and how very right he was in not listening to those who would have dissuaded him from putting a fatal confidence in me. . . Never was there a more delicate nor a stronger friendship between two individuals with so little between them and of so great a difference in age.

This quite unrestrained father-and-son friendship he soon chose to extend to the other members of my family. We have a number of his letters, full of spontaneity, brimming with affection, with gratitude, and with entreaties, when he felt himself too alone in that artificial and unbreathable atmosphere which he had created around himself. We may see here the other side of Surrealist impassivity: "To live, that is to say, to accept life, to laugh, to love, to rejoice, when everything seems so wretchedly bound down . . . in this acceptance lies all there could be in the way of the ridiculous, and our life can only take on a real meaning by setting out from an idea in which it is wholly swallowed up and lost, the moral idea." (*La Révolution surréaliste*, 1929.)

The moral idea harassed Rigaut. He was the most scrupulous of young men. He died from an excess of scruple. The horror of filthiness was in him from his childhood. Let no one be mistaken concerning the purity of his motives when he was engaged in committing "scandalous" and laughable actions, which were no more than the absurd braggadocio of a mild and timid being. He asserted that to ask for a thing instead of taking it constituted an unbearable humiliation. It would seem that he was born humiliated . . . And so, he proceeded to swagger in his dandy's detachment.

But am I not wronging his Legend, that wax-image which he, out of modesty, fashioned of himself? Am I not betraying him by depicting him like other poor flesh-and-blood creatures with eyes for weeping? Our superman, with us, took off his iron girdle. When we reread one of those two pieces which are the only ones he published — upon the first of which Edmond Jaloux had based so many hopes — how can we help being moved by the frankness of the bad boys of the Dada era, of whom Rigaut was the most naïve and the greatest stickler of them all, seeing that he destroyed all his manuscripts. Who is not struck today by the substantial quality of the fragment which appeared in *Littérature* (December, 1920)? ". . . and what a sight, all those people struggling to leave the Gaumont Palace after I had set fire to it! Tonight though, you have nothing to fear, I am in a serious mood. There is obviously not a word of truth in these stories, and I was the best behaved little boy in Paris." Like real revolutionists, Jacques abounded in truculent truisms, which he dressed up in black and shiny velvet, taken out of Hamlet's wardrobe.

Ashamed of his scrawlings upon odds and ends of paper, he would tear them into tiny bits, blow on them and sneer. I am not sure that this was not done out of bitterness, a proud resentment. He felt himself at bottom more a literary man than any one, he who was filled with disgust at the thought of soiling a blank page, and so rigidly

exigent regarding the quality both of the thought and of the form —
he who preferred such absurd pastimes as collecting match-boxes with
pictures of female dancers or guitar-players and other ridiculous trifles.
From ironically observing the stupidity of others, he had contracted
the same mania as a Flaubert being metamorphosed into an Homais
and a Bouvard. Jacques Rigaut was too intelligent not to be alarmed
when he caught sight of himself in the glass-mirror of a skyscraper
corridor, surrounded by millionaires' wives, among whom was his
chosen one.

"I shall be serious, as serious as pleasure. People don't know what
they're talking about. There are no reasons for living, but there are no
reasons for dying either."

(A point of view, alas, which he was one day to abandon.)

"The only means which is granted us to express our contempt for
life is to accept it. Life is not worth the trouble of departing from it.
One may, as an act of kindness, refuse it on behalf of another, but for
oneself? Despair, indifference, betrayals, faithfulness, solitude, family,
liberty, weariness, money, poverty, love, the absence of love, syphilis,
health, sleep, insomnia, desire, impotence, banality, art, honesty,
mediocrity, intelligence — none of these things are worth a damn. We
understand them only too well to pay them any notice; just sufficient
to furnish a few accidental suicides . . ."

From a certain moment on, all the decisions of his day depended
upon a throw of the dice, which he carried around with him.[33] He
played cards, knowing that he would lose: this conviction, which
gradually took hold of his mind, confers a tragic meaning upon the
sudden end which he put to his irritable impatience, to his period of
waiting for the resumption of a conjugal life — and which may have
been, above all, due to that creative work which he felt stirring inside

him, and to which nothing short of a Caesarian operation could have given successful birth. But what was his message? The friend who doubted whether Rigaut had anything of importance to say to us — how sorry he now is for having, in his character "Gonzague" in *La Valise vide*[34], given us a portrait that is disturbing in its external life-likeness, but basically inaccurate, and over which the betrayed model was so pained, although he "laughed a bit nervously" at it all.

There was little of the metaphysician in this youth. If he took himself for a disciple of M. Teste, he impressed me as being just the opposite. When he would bring his Dadaistic comrades to my house, and when I would compare Rigaut's Latin face and American get-up with theirs, I became conscious of the fact that the path he had chosen to follow was not his by instinct. Which would *get* him, Dada or the Ritz? In the meanwhile, I was grateful to him for making me acquainted with some equally remarkable young writers, in whose company it seemed to me that I was once more meeting philosophers, bespectacled professors and neurologists of the sort among whom I had grown up in my grandfather's house. Amid such an Areopagus — the Council of Ten or the Public Health Commission — Jacques' charming *dandysme* was out of place; nevertheless, he was something more than a listener.

Theoretic suicide which was already the mode, and which was to become one of the leit-motifs of Surrealism, had left its funereal mark on him, even to his affectation of "accepting" life of the most conventional and futile sort. He did not align himself with any group. Indeed, he was never more than a spectator at the public performances and public team-play of the Dadaists. But his fantasticality, his attractive singularity should have led them to claim him as one of their own. "He who had humorously conceived the idea of suggesting to rich American families that they have the wooden crosses on the battlefields transformed into marble crosses — he who killed himself on the 5th of November 1929, in an absolutely methodical fashion — he does not expect of us, his friends, those phrases which he himself would have been little disposed to utter over a grave." Such is the chronological notice that appeared in the review conducted by his former comrades.[35]

The question has been raised as to what his production would have been. On his table, shortly before he armed himself with a revolver, a couple of visitors noticed some notebooks — a theatrical piece — if some believed that Rigaut could do nothing, this goes to prove the contrary. He was a psychologist of an astonishing delicacy and subtlety. Would he have written a short denuded novel? With little imagination and no inventiveness as regards plot, being wholly self-absorbed, would he have given his contemporaries an appendix to the *Adolphe* of 1815?

We believe that he had, if not any important messages, at least some very interesting things to say to us, quite as interesting as those uttered by any of his congeners. If we have employed the word *dandy*, this should not shock those who take it in the strict, altogether French sense, of elegant bearing; there are all sorts of dandyisms as there are snobisms; the "demeanour" of Jacques Rigaut toward literature and the amorous life, and in his relations with individuals, was that of a humorist, of one who is making a show of himself.

Certain of us have put to ourselves the question: in what field of present-day life might he have "realized" his character? We are agreed that it would have been in a chosen circle of men and women who were used to his game, and who would have held the key to it. He would have come to it sooner or later, after having kept us waiting some little while. Between cocktails, he would have uttered an amazing phrase, and then would have disappeared like a shadow, satisfied with having produced an exotic impression. For this, on various planes, is the tendency of dandies.

The void he has left behind him shows the number of persons by whom he was looked upon as worthy of being loved.

■ JULIEN TORMA

☐ Julien Torma in
1931.

■ Julien Torma was born in Northern France in 1902 and disappeared in mysterious circumstances in the Tyrol thirty-one years
later. As with Arthur Cravan, biographical information about him is
extremely scarce, especially with respect to his disappearance, and for
this reason the present introduction will draw heavily on the little
which has survived of Torma's correspondence with Max Jacob, René
Daumal and Robert Desnos. The paucity of this information is
further compounded by the fact that Torma, like Jacques Vaché, was
totally unconcerned with forging a literary reputation for himself
either during his own lifetime or for the benefit of posterity. That any
of his writings should have been published at all during his short life
happened less by design than by accident (or, more precisely, as a
result of coincidence) and usually occurred against his better
judgement. Finally, like Rigaut, although on the edge — fairly
unwillingly in Torma's case — of Dada (and later dissident Surrealist)
circles in Paris from the beginning of the 1920s onwards, his ideas
were so nihilistic even by the standards of the epoch that his writing
occasionally assumes a quality which could be mistaken for pastiche
by the unwary. As we shall see, Torma's utter rejection of all forms of
commitment — whether political, social, religious or moral — owes
less to the Parisian Dada milieu than to Alfred Jarry's science of
sciences: pataphysics.

It is hardly surprising, therefore, that the College of Pataphysics has
been active in promoting Torma's work. Indeed, the first reliable
biographical sketch of Torma's life was written by J. H. Sainmont —

■ **Introduction:**
Julien Torma
by Terry Hale

Julien Torma
circa 1922.

who received much, though by no means all, of his information first-hand from Torma's friend Jean Montmort — and published in the *Cahiers* of the College.[36]

Torma's childhood was by no means an easy one. He was born in Cambrai on 6 April 1902. His father died shortly after his birth and his mother, who quickly remarried, died before he was six years old. The young child was then looked after by his stepfather who himself remarried and came to live in Paris, settling permanently at Pontoise in 1916. Between 1909 and 1915, Torma attended school at Batignolles. His stepfather would seem to have been a rather shady character who forced his stepson to run dubious errands for him, including the delivery of drugs.

During his schooldays, as Torma informs us in *Euphorisms*, he made his greatest discovery,"to love his boredom...," and it was also at school that he met Jean Montmort. The latter, as we shall see, would play an important role in his life. It was Montmort, for example, who gathered together and edited Torma's *Euphorisms* — the short collection of aphorisms, translated into English for the first time here — which one commentator has gone so far as to describe as "incomparably more radical and modern than, for example, the annunciation of Gide's *Nourritures Terrestres*."[37]

Julien Torma's first book, *La Lampe obscure*, was published in February 1920 by the proprietor of a small bookshop and publishing house whom the author had met by accident in a café. Torma, by now in his late teens, had just been dismissed from the lowly position he occupied on the local paper, *L'Écho Pontoisien*. The book itself is a collection of erotico-mystical poems owing something (or nothing) in style to the poet Max Jacob whom Torma had met the previous year. In any event, the collection represents an astonishing achievement —

particularly in its use of puns, palindromes, spoonerisms and other devices — for an eighteen year old boy from a broken family.[38] The following example provides some idea, moreover, of the extent to which the mystical and the erotic are fused throughout the work:

□ Julien Torma
circa 1932.

Cataphrase on the Song of Songs

Leave no place empty in my ribs!
Attend to all my holes!
Let the very night be the triumphant sojourn
    of your young eternity,
The belly of Jahveh will be my hunger!
His sex the survival
Of my annihilation.

Max Jacob had converted to Catholicism some ten years earlier, and there is little reason to be surprised that he should have been willing to act as mentor to a young man with a similar mystical tendency as his own. Whatever the extent of Jacob's influence on Julien Torma, the three letters from the former to the latter which have been preserved are of capital importance in tracing the gestation and realisation of *La Lampe obscure*.[39] Over and above such purely literary concerns, however, they also tell the story of the great warmth and affection which existed between these two men — a warmth and affection that Jean Montmort has suggested was not merely platonic.

My Dear Julien,

    I have been casting your birthday horoscope for you. But it isn't ready and I don't want to make a hash of it. There are a number of disturbing aspects, just as there are with you, and I am strongly tempted — by the devil perhaps — to substitute my own

■ **Max Jacob to Julien Torma 5 April 1919.**

for it. It pleases me to be able to inform you that you are destined not to lose your hair. I shall stick at it but am unable to finish it off now. You will continue to compose poetry in the style of Lolo:[40] *trajectory ascendant. There are also some planetary movements. Spiritual trials? I hope so. These are not serious however. We are surrounded by precipices. But that is not why I write. For an Aries, your ram does not bleat very loud nor is it very belligerent: Mars has no part to play in this. I shall not speak, it would be too unorthodox, of the influence of the April Fool so dear to café astrologers. I, sir, am not of their ilk!*

There is much to say respecting the Moon: but she has already made me write so many foolish things. A charming yet baleful element — in astrology as in other things.

My dear Julien, I am terribly sorry that I can't be with you tomorrow. I almost started out for Pontoise. But where could we meet? As I say almost. I hope you will keep your promise to come and see me. With all the Breton ironmongery. Should you forget, I shall be angry at nearly being angry without managing to be.

With best wishes, my dear Julien.

Max

■ Max Jacob to Julien Torma Summer 1919(?).

My Dear Julien,

I am bored and everyone bores me further. There are also those who are trying to irritate me. The holidays are always like that. Fortunately, I have some letters to write. I have written too many letters and am not always sure what I should tell different people. Don't mention this to a soul. You are the only person to whom I can admit such things. You don't believe me perhaps? I can tell that from your letter. You are having a joke at the expense of your Max. But for once I shall not complain, even if I started out that way. It gives me great pleasure to receive such a lot of mail. As a result of repeating these stories I end up believing them all the better myself. Take better *in the best possible sense. Mixing up your correspondents is not always a mistake. It would be utterly charming if they could exchange ever so slightly their personalities. As for me, I would prefer a younger man. You can see me coming. I have held back for you a story that will be not at all to your taste (according to the idea I have of you). Perhaps it is intended for another side of you with which I am less familiar. It's almost real-life à la Zola. The Saint-Malo train meets the Dinard train at Dol. A lady, her son, her mother and their friends climb into a compartment coming from Saint-Malo: "How dare they make passengers coming from Dinard change trains?" she exclaims. It would seem that it would be more practical if the passengers from Saint-Malo had to change trains! "I ask you what could there possibly be in Saint-Malo of any interest at the moment. What a waste of 170 frs. a day at Dinard in order to be forced to change trains. And just look at the compartments! It's outrageous! I shall certain write a letter of complaint to M. Barre, you know: Ferdinand Barre. We shall see. They could at least have warned us that there would be a change. They take your money and when they have no more use for you they just drop you. And what about our friends? Where are they going to sit? We can't even travel with our friends any more! Etc." The story goes on to make the comparison between how expensive life has become and the train on its rails.*

You must write me a long, detailed letter about Lolo. I was disappointed with your last one. You shouldn't joke about such things. I take things seriously. Not seriously enough in my opinion, but more than you do. But it is difficult for me to be serious for two. You deplete my reserves. And that is why I become so maladroit when I take on a reserved air. The heat is quite bearable at the moment. I shall let you know as soon as there is the faintest suggestion of an embryo of a plan to come back. I will wait until then to embrace you. Love me deeply.

    Max

My Dear Julien,

It is inconceivable. First, that you did not find me here. Secondly, that you have not spelled out the truth. What is the meaning of all this? When are you coming back? As you can see, I am writing to you without the slightest delay. Write back in the same way.

I can't help wondering if the Virgin Mary hasn't engineered all this. Especially as I

■ **Max Jacob to Julien Torma 23 October 1919.**

went to confession this morning. And I asked her to protect me for the next 24 hours. She must have listened to my prayers because she knows you inside out. Some things it is better to leave well alone. But I should not say such a thing after my resolutions of this morning. I should start this letter again so that you do not see such unpleasantness. But I shan't do this because if I do I am afraid that you will not see me for the bore that I am. You find everything — me, God — too amusing. And I have been weak enough to let you get away with it and even to encourage you indirectly, just as I do now by not tearing up this letter. My God, I only hope that the sight of my indecision has some purpose. And above all not the outcome that I desire. But I should not write such a prayer after what has gone before it. With you, I am tempted to show myself naked. I am right to say that I am tempted, because it is a temptation.

Lolo will chase it away with a sombre lucidity. I am happy to know that it is coming along. A lamp with claws, like the luminous crabs on the sea-bed. Like them, it occasionally scuttles off at a diagonal. But I shall see for myself by reading through your little packet again. I've had a narrow escape. You still need a good dozen to make a collection. I spotted my olive-tree in the garden.[41] What pleasure you give me! From time to time I need to feel as if I was 18 again. And Cinématoma *bowls me over. Never speak to me again. Do you understand, never! Except to tell me your own pleasure. I'm starting again. Damn! Drop me a line and come soon. I hug you warmly.*

Max

Although copies of *La Lampe obscure* are now extremely sought after (only 200 copies were ever printed), the collection was not a commercial success. Torma, moreover, quarrelled with Jacob (whom he later referred to ironically as "Mob Jacax") soon after the book came out — so depriving himself of potentially his most influential patron. The next few years of Torma's life are particularly sketchy. According to Jean Montmort, his step-parents moved from Pontoise to Paris towards the middle of 1922 and Torma accompanied them there. In any event, he found himself a room in the rue de l'Arbre-Sec almost next door to his publisher and picked up casual work in the nearby market district of Les Halles.

During the course of the next few years, he apparently became friendly with a number of writers associated with the Surrealist movement — including Jacques Rigaut, René Crevel and Robert Desnos — while nonetheless refusing to attach himself to any particular literary group.

La Lampe obscure was followed, in 1925, by another collection of poetry *Le Grand Troche, sorite* (the word *troche*, taken from Nostradamus, means exhaustion or misery while a *sorite* is a chain-syllogism) and, in 1926, an edition of two plays, *Coupures*, a tragedy in nine acts, and *Lauma Lamer*, a one act play. As the title *Coupures* [i.e. *Cuttings*] suggests, the play is in fact made up of lines which have been cut out and juxtaposed at random. That such a technique is highly indebted to Dada is self-evident, though the feeling of disorientation which is achieved is less a matter of incoherence in the immediate sense, as was frequently the case with Dada, and more to do with the manner in which the assumptions of the theatre are systematically undermined or shown to be inadequate. The central protagonist of *Coupures*, for example, is a certain Osmur, described in the text as an ancillary son of the god Jupiter but more clearly recognisable as a phonetic anagram of *surhomme* (or superman). This ominous figure maintains a running commentary on the entries and exits of the various characters, their gestures, and what they say — thereby underlining the absurdity not only of the action but also of the dialogue.[42]

On his twenty-fourth birthday (6 April 1926), Julien Torma sent Robert Desnos a copy of *Coupures* and *Lauma Lamer* accompanied by the following letter. Desnos at the time was still an active member of the Surrealist movement — indeed, he had recently completed *La Liberté ou l'amour!* [tr. *Liberty of Love!*, Atlas Press], generally considered as one of the masterpieces of early Surrealism — though his relationship with Breton was becoming increasingly strained in the light of the latter's disapproval of further activity in the domain of automatic writing.

■ **Julien Torma to Robert Desnos, Meaux, 6/4/25.**[43]

My Dear Desnos,

I have enclosed some claptrap of mine. Do not sit on it too long. The theatre of tomorrow, as august personages say, will lack grandeur without our little bomb. I bet you a pound of diplodocus shit — and you know how much this costs as well as you know the lightness of wallet of an employee of the Publicateur de Seine-et-Marne *— if you crack it.*

I have just been hatching a scheme concerning the Revolt of words — model October 1917 — and there is something to get really excited about in the verbal catastrophe (style tautologically restrained) I see here. But I'm too tired to copy it again tonight.

Any chance of meeting up?

J. Torma

1926 also saw the publication of *Euphorisms*, a collection of notes and fragments assembled by Jean Montmort (who also paid for the printing) and dedicated to René Crevel. If Torma's earlier work still suggested an occasional hint, if not of sympathy, then at least familiarity with Parisian Dada or French Surrealism (one of the poems in *Le Grand Troche*, for example, alludes to Breton and Soupault's *The Magnetic Fields*), then *Euphorisms* passes beyond any such affiliation and is his most radical work. Indeed, so great is the author's refusal to commit himself to any system of thought that his derision and irony extends even to Dada. *Euphorisms* attacks the very root of reason not by rejecting such notions as truth, knowledge, or intelligibility but by refusing to accept their desirability. So much so that when, in *Euphorisms*, Torma is called upon to define his own position — or non-position — he can only refer to Jarry and the science of pataphysics. This he does on innumerable occasions. Many of these points are well exemplified in the correspondence between Julien Torma and René Daumal.[44]

In October 1925 Daumal had been sent to the prestigious Lycée Henri-IV in Paris to prepare the entrance examination to the Ecole Normale Supérieure. It was at the beginning of this period of quasi-exile from his friends and future collaborators in *Le Grand Jeu* that Daumal met Julien Torma. The first letter was presumably written shortly before Daumal returned to Reims for the Christmas holiday.

My Dear Torma,

I have been thinking over what you said yesterday. There's a lot that needs clarification. But that shouldn't deter us from trying to see a way through. Or should that be the other way round?

That chap at H. IV you'd heard of isn't called Borne by any chance? He fits the description you gave pretty well and he isn't very bright. Not that that matters very much. I don't think there's anything brewing in that direction. He's the sort of fellow who always makes two and two add up to four. I'm sure he was perfectly sincere when he gave me a nought for the fresher's essay which, as an experiment, I had composed in the manner of the Surrealists.

Rest assured that I am as conscious of your respectability as the first words we exchanged about the quays. Joking apart, would you like me to do something about that next Thursday? Or can it wait until January?

See you soon in any case.

René Daumal

■ **René Daumal to Julien Torma 11 December 1925.**

The following year, Daumal came across a copy of *La Lampe obscure* on one of the bookstalls on the Paris quays. Torma, for reasons which are explained in a letter to Robert Desnos (*infra*), had deliberately neglected to inform him of the existence of this early collection of his poetry. Daumal twisted Torma's arm to write him a long dedication. Torma's reluctance, mentioned earlier, to participate in any kind of literary movement is clearly evident from the following letter addressed to René Daumal. Unfortunately, the first page is missing. This letter may be dated, however, around the period in which Daumal and Roger Gilbert-Lecomte were preparing *Le Grand Jeu*. Torma refused to be drawn into the group:

■ **René Daumal to Julien Torma, 6 April 1925.**

... intentions. You know what Lecomte and I think of you and the ascendancy which your culturelessness has given you. We can undertake nothing without you. The very fact that you turned Roger down flat bestows upon you personally the principal weight of the void. There is a force about you which is bewildering because it rests on nothing.

It is this nothing which is precious.

You are quite right to dissociate yourself from La Lampe obscure, *its dark lucidity flared up once and for all in the midst of the colourless fogs. And in disowning it, you also affirm it, just as in creating it you exceeded what you were writing or you were exceeded by it. You maintain that even as a gilded youth you smiled at the incredibly farcical and distracted language. Others have experienced that. But do you know if you were the master of your instrument? Who was speaking? What if the irony which you thought you had secreted within was not a sign added to all the others, leading to the denunciation of the unintelligible ballast of the soul? The Lamp no longer belongs to you and its shine reflects a World in my eyes which I know only too well.*

We have other friends who also know the work. But they know nothing about you yet. We did not wish to appear to have pledged you to their way of thinking even by simple presumption. And if you "persist" in this, neither Roger nor myself will do you a "wrong."

Make no mistake. We need neither a leader nor a prophet. What we need is this ballast. One can never have too great a void inside oneself. If you keep your distance, at least act as a myth: that could not displease you.

I cannot help wondering why you refuse to see Breton. Roger, like everyone else, does not stand up to him as he should. I can guess what will happen. What we need from you first is an answer. Best wishes,

    René

In July 1929, the second issue of the review *Bifur*, edited by Georges Ribemont-Dessaignes (who had recently been excluded from the Surrealist movement by André Breton), published an article by René Daumal entitled: *La Pataphysique et la révélation du rire*. Having procured Torma's address from Jean Montmort, Daumal sent him a copy accompanied by the following letter. Both this letter and Torma's reply make detailed reference to this article.[45]

My Dear Julien,

After many a summer, I wanted to resurface for you, sure that you would welcome these pages of pataphysical apocalypse. I got your address from J.M., not without twisting his arm (I mention this so that you won't be too hard on him) for he only gave in after I told him what it was about. He led me to understand that you no longer write any poetry, or rather, because I can imagine the shock these insane thoughts will cause you, that, without ever having given the time of day to these colonisers, you used to give the impression of playing with them when the song appealed to you but that now the music's over. Is that the best way of putting it?

Forgive me for having sent you Bifur? *I have no idea what your reactions are. Bad?*

■ **René Daumal to Julien Torma, [undated].**

Or will you dash through it snapping the pages? You will laugh if I speak of your severity and say purely and simply that you couldn't care less. Purity and simplicity. I will run the risk, however, not for the sake of Bifur, *nor even for that of Pataphysics, but for you whom I still miss and whom I would have liked to accompany further along the roads of this planet:*

> *What cruel arm restrains me here,*
> *Fugitives of the World, while North you flee.*[46]

With Roger we invoke you from time to time from behind the veil. You know that we are getting on more than ever with Le Grand Jeu *and facing up to all the indispensable problems. More recently, we recalled the years when your presence meant so much for us — and something different from what you would have wished. These enterprises beyond measure which we urge on with all our strength and which you perhaps do not approve of fill our entire lives and occasionally make us dream of what we had hoped of you. Write back to me and tell me what you are doing and what you are writing.*

> *Best wishes,*
> *René*

■ **Julien Torma to René Daumal, Lille, 20 October 1929**

My Dear Daumal,

No apologies needed for sending the issue of Bifur. Bifur *is* Bifur, *and you may daub things on walls if you have a mind to. You were right to send a copy as I would not have got to hear of your article otherwise — and discovered that pataphysics could be married to mysticism. I am still intrigued by that. Of all the reading matter that chance has thrown in my way — and that worthy deity has always done well by me — the various pieces that I have come across by Jarry have always seemed the least tedious to me. I see by way of them. There are those who see by way of H. Bourdeaux or Gide. Is there anything wrong with that? As for me, I see through the eyes of Sengle or Emmanuel Dieu*[47]. *Question of taste and pretentions. Indeed, it is even what makes some books still possible, because I am no longer — despite your past remonstrances —*

interested in either culture or gnosis. So I am pleased to find you seeing via the same bodies of smoke.

Once again I shirk the issue.

It will come as no surprise to learn that I do not much care for your slaps of the absolute, having little faith in any other kind of absolute except that which slaps. Is there any other? I found your article upsetting because everything in it is true. Except the tone. The word true means precisely nothing here and succumbs under a pataphysical paw-swipe. You are right to speak of chaos. But one gets the feeling that you believe in it as if it were some sort of God. In spite of your subtlety, my dear René, you have too much of the graciousness-of-god about you. You are working at the absolute.

Your pataphysician laughs too much. And that laughter is both too comic and too cosmic. Put metaphysics behind pataphysics and you make it merely the facade for a belief. Now the essence of pataphysics is that it is the facade of a facade, behind which there is nothing.

I do not see Dr Faustroll laugh. I do not have the book to hand. But I would swear blind — don't you see? — How can you write: "Faustroll grins." You are horribly behind the times. We are no longer at the Méphisto stage. At evil and guilty consciences, or even consciences at all. If Faustroll turns Mephistophelian it can only be part of a pataphysical game. Because Mephistophelianism is something they cooked up, as we were saying. Faustroll is imperturbable. Or not at all. He has the appearance of being natural and of not being natural. Because nature is just one more farce neither more nor less interesting than another. He does not choose, he no longer distinguishes, he no longer prefers. He voyages wrong side up. But his voyage does not even exist. These characters and their adventures are not real. This is clearly seen in the death and the resurrection of Bosse-de-Nage. But neither are they imaginary in the sense of the heroes of novels and stories in the fantastic genre. One supposes, provisionally at least, however extravagant the hypothesis, that it is not totally implausible that those heroes exist. But it is pretty rich of you to say that all defined existence is a scandal. With the One and suchlike. But why not say that undefined existence is a scandal, though the *word scandal is superfluous. Faustroll says: "I am God," and he surely has as much right to say that as does God himself. All the same it is a bit much — or not much enough — to take him seriously.*

No writing — either holy or impeeous — No time to. I am doing nothing, just boring jobs, and jobbing boredom. It will go on like zat... (or sade) *probably till our dying day. So be it — Do not take that as an alluvion* (sic)*.*

All the usual ... best

    Torma

Did R.D. (the other one) *tell you I almost spoke ill of you to him six months ago? He wrote to say he was not among the tortillionnaires.*[48]

After the publication of *Euphorisms*, Julien Torma would appear to have written little more. His life for the next five years would be one of perpetual drifting. For a week sometime in 1926 he worked as an unskilled labourer for a firm in Charleville, the birthplace of Arthur Rimbaud. In 1929, he was to be found in Lille. Robert Desnos managed to unearth him.

■ **Julien Torma to Robert Desnos, Lille, 11 March 1929.**

My Dear Desnos,

You have had the most incredible good fortune in tracking down my address — but there is nothing I can tell you of any great interest about what you want to know.

I got to know Daumal a very long time ago when he was still at Henri IV. He would meet me on Sunday at the Rendez-vous des amis. *I liked him because he was interested in pataphysics. A curious coincidence: he came across one of my offspring — one, fortunately, that you haven't read,* La Lampe obscure *— by accident on the quays. I was seventeen when I wrote it and spending quite a bit of time with Mob Jacax. It seems funny now. But there was already something of a salutatory ambiguity about it! In any event, my friend Daumal took a real shine to it and practically forced me to inscribe a little screed in it. I well remember it because I am extremely reluctant* *even to even touch the book, and despite this I ended up explaining to him that even for the young idiot who wrote it the book meant the opposite of what it said. Far from turning him against it, this seemed to excite him, and I suspected him of lapsing into mysticism — not unintelligently, mark you, but sceptically, though still taking himself devilishly seriously. I cannot help but find it amusing that that has been my only literary influence (greetings fellow* littérateur*). Indeed, he showed me some poems which had been inspired by it. And he even had the nerve to tell me that he found* La Lampe obscure *the best thing I had done. But then he has never seen me make love. Anyway, all that is without much importance.*

Shortly after this Daumal brought his friend Lecomte, who was living at Reims or Nancy with his mammoth-like parents, to see me. Very O. The lad seemed to me to take himself for a prophet. I didn't like that much. So I washed out his head a bit. The pair of them seemed to have faith in oriental salads. It all seemed infernally divine to me. Faced with my refusal, Lecomte anointed me superior and pretended to hold me for a prophet. Was he just pulling my leg or did he really believe it? In any event, they didn't take me in and I handed him the enclosed little piece of paper that I found in an old notebook.[49] *He felt very let down and I hardly saw him again. Daumal still came round regularly, though a little less often, right until I left for Paris.*

I know almost nothing about Le Grand Jeu *and have even less interest.*

I imagine that you intend to torment these two youngsters. That will teach them to mess with the Church. I can be a right bastard here.

What's life like? Nothing worth telling. Stupid. As for belles-lettres, *I'm tending to steer clear of them since the* Euphorisms *coup. No time to write anyway.*

Shake a leg, my old mate.

Unwesternly.

J. Torma

Torma was once again in Lille towards the Easter of 1932 after trips to Brussels and Antwerp and a six month stay in Rouen. It was there that he met Philippe Merlen whose letter, reprinted later in this work, casts considerable light on Torma's life at about this time. In November 1932, Torma's health gave way and he wintered in a guest house at the foot of the Wildespitze in the Tyrol. He disappeared while on a solitary walk in the mountains on 17 February 1933. His body was never recovered.

☐ Portrait of Torma by Max Jacob, and left: the last photograph of Torma, the Tyrol, 1933.

■ One should not let the cat out of the bag before it has been skinned.   ■ **Euphorisms**[50]

Why not speak THEIR language, stupid blockhead? It's the best way to take the piss and the only one that is really *in bad taste.* Isn't sacrilege the worst of all "crimes"?

Sacrilege is acceptable only as a game. It doesn't just miss the target, it winds up cancelling itself out.

Religious sacrilege, for example imitates the outward appearance of an act of devotion: otherwise, it must be added, the priest would refuse communion; therefore one commits sacrilege only for oneself since, in the eyes of others, it is just an act of conformism: in other words, merely a matter of getting up God's nose. All the same, we haven't yet got that far! If pure sacrilege involves faith in that which it defies, it is   ■ **Counter-key**
not really sacrilege — and believers know they need atheists of the type of Sébastien Faure[51] (as God has need of the Devil).

The sacrilege that is truly sacrilegious is unselfconscious and *ambiguous* — like beauty. And it is more amusing.

Thought involves a little charlatanism.

It is not *natural* to think: one must create a veritable stage-setting out of oneself and things, not to mention the inevitable artificial device of reasoning . . . Without these shams, thought is no more than naïveté (banging on about the obvious) and, basically, stupidity. Intelligence involves deception as speech does lying.

Better to admit frankly to this rule of the game and do knowingly what everyone else does unknowingly. Deliberately inject into one's thought the element of charlatanry required for it to be thought, rather than oneself be its dupe. In this way one can vary the dosage *as one pleases*. Cagliostro was a thinker; Nietzsche's weak point was perhaps (?) to be unaware of the Cagliostro in himself.

The strange initiation into language.

The first cries are no more than mechanical effects produced by the functioning of the body. Even the first words are still not *words*. The child discovers autonomous reality only by lying. Then the word is used for itself; it becomes meaning. Game or chance, it matters little: the child says "*bobo*," "hurt." Right away (and even if it hasn't felt any

■ **Soul's kick**[52]   pain) the whole sequence of cajoleries and sugary consolations is triggered off. It is understandable that, after this discovery, the child tries the experiment again, the better to assure itself of the wonderful efficacy of the Word. And if it loves lying so much (that joy in its eyes), that is because it is savouring the happiness and the power of the cabalistic intelligence: the word is creative.

It is by this devious utterance that the "truth" is expressed.

Believing in the spirit. As if one needed to! People still believe too much in it — above all the "materialists" (who indulge in science, that is to say blindly exalt the power of the spirit). What is needed is to believe, energetically, tenaciously, passionately, with the faith that moves mountains, in the body.

We suppose we expend our energy in gesticulations, but it is it that expends us in alms in the begging-bowl of the blind.

The reflexes of life persist for some time among the guillotined. —
So? — That ought to "console" you, since you feel the need to survive . . .

" . . . *Regarding those who are saddened by the inevitable necessity of death, let them be
consoled by the promise of a future immortality.*"
    But those it does not sadden?

Our ideas about death are ingenuous. Some believe we do not die.
That is — obviously — too naïve. Others believe that dying is *nothing*,
that before, one lives, and afterwards one no longer gives it any
thought. That is — no less obviously — too well thought out. It
seems, should one wish to judge it coldly, that it is the latter who are
in the right, because it is they who better express the facts. But this is
an illusion: facts here say nothing, if they *ever* say anything. Death.
Death is ironic.

■ **The *I*s are cast**

Man is an onion, the noblest there is in nature, but a peeling onion —
like any other.
    A skin? You don't know how right you are.
    But, if you remove it, you'll find another, and another . . . down to
the void at the centre (that's not all that large, either).
    Let's weep, let's weep,
    My crocodile brothers.

From my window: "the everyday horizon of roofs." My I-roofs.[53]
    — If I were me.

We say *suspect* to mean suppose. That which is hypothetical is *accused*:

why not clear enough to be immediately obvious? We consider as a sort of betrayal or a vague threat that ambiguity of the world which — cocking a snook, we suspect, at Kant — makes a mockery of us.

■ The World's minus

But I, who make a mockery of the World, I equally suspect supposition, supposer and suppository, calving cow and veterinarian. They're in cahoots, they're in on the secret: without knowing it. And I too, although I know it. That's why I can tip my invisible winks.

The object is that which is objected against me.

The world is a tapestry whose reverse, variegated with hanging threads and whip-stitches, is the poem. When one has had a quick look BEHIND, one cannot prevent oneself having this in mind while looking at the right side.

The problem of pupae.

On a train, at night, the situation is clear. It's a matter of choosing: either to look at one's neighbours, or else to peer closely at what's outside.

Yet there are those who reckon also to see a relation between the two.

Nature is only another chimera.

■ April fool

My opinion of nature:

The feet try in vain to tempt the ground; it is a sated belly, refusing all superfluity. Who would dare brag of doing as much?

Whiteness is filthy.

Nothing astounds me more than the taste of the commonalty for dogs, cats, parrots, etc. For my part, a creature interests me only when its reactions become totally alien to me. The leech isn't too bad, the starfish is quite an improvement. But slugs! Speak to me of slugs![54]

Society is a concert (with its bum-notes, of course). But people are disconcerting. To reassure oneself, one pretends to confound them. People talk of the *"beau monde,"* or of "mixing in high society." Cosmic— and comic — *demi-monde.*

Demon is the anagram of *monde.*

The unexpected is not all that so. Fortunately, it would otherwise go unrecognised and pass unnoticed. Tediously, it is for this very reason that it quickly becomes tedious.

I don't know whether there are numbers. And you?

We are mistaken in not being on our guard against certain ill-effects of thought. I take it as understood that a pleasant event will take place only at the moment when I am giving it the least thought, and because I am giving it the least thought. The thought kills the event, and from the still-born event there arise mortal emanations. Action, that is to say *creation*, constitutes the exact inverse of conscious thought. In that second I kill in myself something a thousand times better than my thought. Let's think no more, *dis-pense* with thinking.[55]

■ **March hare**

Forgetting is the most living thing there is in life. The secret of magical renewal and of *virtù*, valour, strength. Reconciliation too is the *only* solution, the solution of continuity.

In illness, it is the memory that usurps and invades the living being: the body is *marked* and cannot, at least for a while, efface the trace of a dreadful past. Death is the *subversive* subversion of all forgetting. Since cohesion is maintained only by the onward impulse, total fixation is at the same time decomposition. And the corpse, when it becomes past, returns to its own past, that is to say to the beginning of the cycle, to the original elements. In the consciousness of the dying man this finds expression in the well known hypermnesia under which it falls apart.

Forgetting is thus still the panacea, the remedy in the absence of a remedy: the veritable potable gold of alchymical science. *And I lived a* golden *star by the light of nature*. Forgetting is yellow, as Van Gogh SAW it. Hence the melancholy of memory and the moralistic-pallbearer mannerism that takes hold of all those who live *in the past.*

Not life, but a fit-up between life and death.

■ *Credo* **on credit**

Yes, Monsieur, I'm a schizoid, and even a schizophrenic. Moreover, if I haven't, properly speaking, an Oedipus complex, I certainly have a superiority complex (especially as regards the likes of you). A touch of dementia, with a disintegrative tendency and agoraphobia, an anal fixation, etc. And apart from that? Is that really all?

As for you, who — evidently — a doctor whose treatments are sound, you are — no less evidently — a stupid jerk.

Believers are stupid because, if they were intelligent, they would already have the stupidity of hypocrisy.

The hypocrite, in effect, despite the prodigious resources he must on occasion display, winds up believing in the value of his simulation.

One then gets an inkling of the ontological consistency of the treacly mess in which believers splash about. It is probably upon this that they base their experience of the infinite. But they are to be found elsewhere than in the churches.

There are those who give no thought to believing and those who discover that they believe. The first are the *real believers*, like savages or sorcerers. The others are Jesuits or intellectuals, all the *cooks* who prepare the desserts of certitude.

Those who dare to admit that they believe know perfectly well that one cannot believe them. If they dig their heels in, we witness the usual desperate attempts (with frenzied manifestations): the Catholicism of Péguy (who, moreover, did not get himself baptised), the fascist psychosis, the Bolshevik "dialectic," and, in a general way, the agitation of all those ranters who suppose they are bringing about the "good." Science is an opium which is less maligned, but which is the most disappointing, except to the bureaucrats of the *believed*.

■ **A thesis for atheists**

You are still caught up in the temptation of Anthony. The twitch of zeal curtailed, the tics of puerile pride, dejection and terror . . .

Knowing is always more or less pretending to know. It can be interesting, on occasion, to observe the learned, that useless and conceited species.

After having been the terrorists' bomb of revolt and doubt, science is on the point of becoming (*is already*) an implacable instrument for maintaining order.

One sees this in the *tone* of all those tin-pot science-mongers: they will be worse than the inquisitors, and religious obscurantism will have been an Eden compared with scientific obscurantism.

The old scientism, naïve and optimistic, harmless on account of its stupidity, was in no way comparable to this new dogmatism which believes itself called upon to legislate on everything, society, morals, art, thought (when one imagines oneself *in possession* of the truth...), which already exerts censorship by the Index of its contempt, and which before long will make use of the secular arm after having provided it with effective resources.

■ **Percolator of the absolute**

The reason why science so readily turns keen-witted and even free-thinking minds into imbeciles is that, despite everything, it is in part true.

In all those history-based doctrines there is something, I don't know what, sexagenerically simplistic. Constipated and pretentious. Missions and vocations. In the name of an "evolution," which in reality is no more than the kiddies' scooter of their little *Weltanschauung*, they invent the future and call upon us to sacrifice ourselves for it. And their solemnity.

Yet history is such a curious and rankly fertile example of the work of forgers! No doubt they regret their lack of awareness; it would be a bit much if all that had been wrapped up in advance. And the historians are the very opposite of those *playing a game*. At the very most they cheat for a "cause," for "the good," they are incapable of cheating for cheating's sake.

But if we consider the farcical puppet-show that is the result of their conscientious, virtuous, scientific faking — it must be admitted that it's not so bad after all.

Importance is unimportant.

The genius of the drunk. He reasons, and demonstrates his drunkenness. But reasonings and demonstrations are of no interest because they are false.

The âme, *the "soul" of a cannon: the hole into which the charge is placed.* (Littré).

■ Parlour games

We were playing a game which, seen in the perspective of the times, seems to me pretty disturbing. Speaking to our local Joseph Prudhomme and Homais[56], we pretended to take them for formidable deadpan jokers, playing this last thirty years at taking the piss out of the bourgeoisie: we saw through their game and were claiming the honour of becoming their accomplices. The faces they pulled, the misunderstandings! And then (that's where the trouble begins) we still weren't at all sure who was fooling and who was being fooled. One of them, defrocked, a scientist and a patriot — hallucinating — had a way of looking at me as he was saying *"we"* that was literally frightening. It went, in all probability, far beyond the most inspiring hypocrisy. The man coming, it goes without saying, five minutes later, to shit on things that as like as not were better.

THEY imagine that the schizophrenic, repudiating the universe you know, installs himself in another. As if that were all. But the schizophrenic who does not talk a lot of hot air gets round shamefully to fooling his keepers. By dint of his schizophrenia he winds up emerging from it, and sees no better way of holding up this filthy world to ridicule than by treating it as the Perfect Kingdom. Finally, it has for him no importance whatever.

We point this out to the competent psychiatric authorities and urge them to specify in their rules that: 1) Such a schizophrenic is a dangerous madman; 2) Every individual in good health and normally constituted must have in their thought, if not in their acts, a proportion of the ideal that might be fixed at about 22%.

I am *also* that shadow that follows me and which I flee.

■ Oneirical uncle[57]

Shadow of a shadow, dancing on the ramshackle walls of chance, to the point of *preceding* me during those moments when the heat on my back dissolves me in the sight of that frenzied caricature which frightens me too much for me to laugh to my heart's content.

Dream. I was damned. Along with those who were in the same situation, one exited to the left. Then a labyrinth of corridors. We came to a sort of hospice. Fairly well organised. They sorted us out among rooms which it *appeared* we could not leave. I say *appeared* because nowhere was this specifically laid down. Uniformed guards were going about, very polite, always ready to be of service — but naturally there was no service to ask of them. Was it perhaps their presence that prevented one from leaving? Nothing, at all events, of the traditional hell. There were three of us in my room. A fellow, well-built as regards his person, blond and slim, with intelligent eyes, and a woman, a brunette wearing a voluminous yellow dress which, I have no idea why, filled me with delight. I said to myself: "Devil take it (hmm), I'm not dreaming" (I often say that in my dreams), "whatever this is, it isn't the hell of the *curés*, it must be the real one." For all that, this observation did rather bother me: I was vaguely irritated that I, being what I am, should be brought to admit the existence of a hell (while reflecting thus I even momentarily forgot I was there). I suddenly thought: "I really wish this were a dream." At the same time I saw clearly by my *embarrassment* in the presence of my companions for eternity that things were going to turn out badly. The woman was beginning to make up to me in a thoroughly indecent manner. I protested that I admired only her dress. She said: "So this is hell, then? It's going to be great if you admire my dress for all eternity without wanting to go to bed with me! Let's at least rush headlong into depravity, needle Him Up There." — "Who's that?" I said, looking at our companion, who seemed to be furiously angry. "Idiot." she replied. "And on top of that you're holding back." — "You know very well our bodies are spiritualised," I said, fully aware of the imbecility of invoking that theology. The woman accused me of wanting to seduce the blond young man: at the end of my tether, I replied that I'd gladly do so if only to annoy her (I nevertheless had the feeling of making a blunder to be avoided at all costs). I no longer know what he interjected, but the atmosphere was very tense, so much so that I said to myself: "It's *really* like it is on earth" — then, suddenly: "But it's idiotic! They've conned us. This is symbolic, it's *liberal protestantism!*" I can vouch for this last formula which filled me with an invincible horror as regards my stupidity, and that all the more so since the effective presence of that embarrassing flare-up was still very much on my mind. This violent disgust awoke me.

■ **Wish soup**

Dream. I am on a train. My neighbours are eating thick sandwiches. I have a bout of nausea: I tell myself I've eaten too much *paté de foie* between meals. (N.B. that I never eat it, and that, in any case, I never eat between meals.) The train stops in the middle of nowhere. A woman gets down on to the track. I say: "Don't you commit suicide," thinking at the same time that I'm being ridiculous and that I'd never say that *in reality*. Where am I, then? I want to vomit, and to be on my way. Yet I know that as long as that woman isn't dead, the train won't start. Never mind. I vomit out of the window: there and then, the train starts; the woman runs along behind. I tug on the alarm-bell. *Dreadful noise.* All the travellers come running. It's stifling. "The situation is absurd," I tried to explain. But people respond by pointing at me in a threatening manner. "You won't be making any more trouble." Scuffle. Utter confusion. I'm thrown out of the window.

■ Asbestos G-string

Dream. In a telephone booth in Les Halles. I'm waiting for a call from who knows whom and who knows where. A tinkling bell, comparable to those of altar-boys. I lift the receiver. At the end of the line, amidst the fizzling sound of a Bickford fuse (at the same time, the idea of an enormous impending danger), I catch the minuscule sound of a kiss imprinted on fingertips. Then nothing more. Ringing again. The same again, three or four times. Suddenly a voice which seems to be coming from below the panelling. A harmonious voice, a bit muffled. It is speaking in an unknown foreign language, rich in vowels, with a very marked tonic accent. I listen to this voice with an increasingly passionate interest. It becomes undeniable that my whole life depends on the words that are oozing out of the wall. That voice (by no means the impression of not understanding the *meaning* of what is being said, although the words — I'm aware of that — remain hermetic to me) is filling me with a sense of euphoria which I suddenly discover is essentially erotic. I press my abdomen against the panelling of the booth. Ringing. Without my picking up the instrument, I hear the fizzling of the Bickford fuse, then, a second later, a *resounding fart* accompanied by a deafening burst of abominably vulgar laughter. I then awaken progressively, shot through by a series of more or less instantaneous images. Indefinable persons pitying my fate: just time to grasp the fact that the telephone has announced the rejection of my plea for clemency and that I can extricate myself only by means of a first-rate witticism. I search in vain for some witticism. The fizzling of the Bickford fuse. Then the voice from the panelling suddenly whispers to me no end of amusing things which go right through me without coming to rest. Then, becoming more and more jumbled, in an increasingly jeering tone, the voice recites a poem, extremely classical in style and extraordinarily pornographic.

■ **The ultra-clairvoyant**

Dream. A woman of about thirty, brunette, wearing a blood-red suit, is about to pass me on the pavement of a violently sunlit street. Deserted. I wish to turn back, or at least to cross the street. But, as it happens, I want to see what's going to happen. Suddenly, at the moment she draws level with me, she throws herself upon me, very nimbly, and kisses me on the right side of my throat. A disagreeable sensation I can't describe. For the sake of saying something, I say: "I could really do with a drink." But she withdraws, and, lo and behold, her lips remain stuck to my throat (or is it the skin of my throat that remains stuck to her lips?), and between the two of us a disgusting filament stretches out, stretches out, for she makes off rapidly. Help-lessness and repulsion. I await the snapping of that revolting elastic-like object. So over-excited that I awake without knowing whether it has broken.

Dream. A labyrinth of dark corridors spiralling downwards. Intestinal landscape. Impression that I'm going to go on walking like this for eternity. How to get out? We carry on downwards (I say *we* because there's an absolute crowd thronging in these corridors, but, in reality, all the time it's me). Luxuriously comfortable cinemas as well as immense urinal-cathedrals, feebly illuminated by neon open off these sinuosities. The ground underfoot gives the impression of walking on

■ Brain blow-out a raft of dropsical bellies. A whiff of sea-breeze reaches me at the precise moment I realise that I am in a penal colony, condemned to forced labour for life.

Short of being a shopkeeper or serious, one cannot but pull up short, faced with the *real-unreal* distinction, conspicuous in the quack-quack of common sense.

The first to admit it — of course — are the defenders of the marvellous, would-be schizophrenics (the modern Diogenes in search of a real one). Their opium no longer has any effect. They pretend to believe in it, but nobody is taken in. Not even they themselves.

Inside-out schizophrenics, our head-to-tail, spade-headed realists are the real cripples vis-à-vis that which does not *concern* them. Let us bear in mind the sexually pathological element in that mental illness (commonly called *common sense*).

So? It's very simple. To succeed, sell the real or the unreal. Be a banker or a poet. A superficial difference.

Otherwise there's only failure.

It was in arithmetic-books that I grasped the stupidity of posing problems. For me, who ran all my step-parents' errands, it was a doddle (and a guaranteed success) to point out to the teacher the falsity of all those "supposes" invented for the sake of inventing them. Since then I have discovered that problems *are not even* false problems.

A maudlin sham, stitched up in difficulties, and which consists in trying to reconcile that which one has previously painstakingly separated. The World and the Spirit, the Plenum and the Void, work and rest . . . Practices which are scarcely of any interest except to those who don't have a living to make. For life — true or false — takes good care to water down the dialectical poison into the PHENOUMENON.[58]

■ Headcheese[59]

The contrary of the problem is the poem.

To get one's suspicions' backs up: the end and means of the poem. I also suspect the poem itself, and even that suspicion.

Poetry is an idea *x*.

The physiognomy of the head and that of the hands, notwithstanding their (fairly spicy) element of the con-trick, have come in the end to colour the most *everyday* experience, which for all that winds so weary a way . . . But their failing is to have us regard the rest of the body as of no importance.

Knees, for example. Whilst other painters and sculptors turned out knees in a mass-production fashion, Michelangelo, who nevertheless had *his own type* of knee, varied it to infinity. He who would weep with admiration at the lateral apparition of three ribs at a raising of the arms, knew his knees as he did his alphabet.

As much could be said of the buttocks which, to the practised eye, should be as eloquent as the face — and even more so: for in a face there are so many divergent signs, hence a certain difficulty in arriving at a synthesis of it, whilst the vision, the perception of buttocks boils down to the grasping of a few lines in their inflexions and a few masses

■ Colourless danger

in their modelling: it is at once more stylised and more harmonious, therefore easier to grasp — although every bit as subject to variations.

And the front-side is as psychologically subtle as the backside.

But in a society that has managed to police itself only by becoming a police-society, we run scarcely any risk of superseding the *fiche anthropométrique*,[60] that noble conquest of modern genius, for which, down the centuries, a whole humanity of informers, spies and cops have sighed, and which is well on its way to making itself felt as the *last word* in Knowledge.

Real intimacy (the only one) is body-to-body.

Thinking one's thought through to the end, what else is that than running up against one's mental limits and killing one's thought by having it smash its skull against the bars of its cage? Or that being the case, to content oneself with *taking a stroll round one's estate*, going round in circles — *"mors-toi la queue, serpent?"*[61] In any case thought leads to nothing other than to itself, and all roads lead to man: thought is a bourgeois pastime. A reflection which is, after all, perfectly bourgeois, and it is also entirely frivolous. To understand, to despair, or to remain silent, is always an act of faith of a kind, a way of settling down, of resting on one's despair or one's silence.

■ Reason gives no credit

Lighting up the night only makes it more obvious.

Getting oil out of the wall to grease the snail's palm.

Living is a kind of hide-and-seek. In seeking out ideas, men, and one-self, one reckons to have a pretext for not getting lost or, at all events, in the masked ball in which we are carried along, to find one's clothes again in the cloakroom.

It's not the light that's attracting me, but the darkness that's driving me on.

They bang on about the obvious, want to cover it in thick layers so as no longer to see the *obscure*, and, after pages of equations, finally get down to formulating $0 = 0$.

   I (and I state it with all necessary pride) like roads leading nowhere and featureless, pathless countrysides, I dissect the inevident, I grill the incidental, I relish the fortuitous, and, at the very end of my zig-zagging, I take pleasure in formulating, for example: Paul Claudel (or whatever you like) $= Q$.[62]

You wouldn't be looking for me if you hadn't already found me. — So it's only a game of hide-and seek?
   —You believed that, you greenhorn?

SANDWICH GOD.   ■ **God of straw**

Those who speak of Nothingness take good care not *to go and see it*. But they'd be a good deal more careful, for fear of losing their (rather dodgy) business and their *raison de non-être*, if they knew what it is, because it isn't even a load of eyewash, it's a privy. Exactly like the Absolute, its twin brother.

Hunger justifies the middle classes.

As near as makes no difference, all martyrs have the look of perjurers about them. Very well pleased that they're taken seriously. But it's no use dying, you've got to suffer to a nicety. And, if that weren't enough, it never proves anything.

Chance? Its creations are no more unsuccessful than those of the Other. Its intentions are every bit as unpredictable, its power infinite. It resembles him like a brother. Like him, it indulges itself in improvisations, its sublimity likewise is a trifle hackneyed: one shouldn't take what pans out unduly seriously. Like God, a procurer and a murderer: and a pushover, open to *all comers.*

■ **The Bonfire of the Palliatives**

    One can even hand over decisions to it. We are so stupid and mulish that, being indifferent, it is necessarily wiser. And, compared to our bolster of an imagination, it's quite simply "marvellous." Heads or tails, *sortes a Deo veniunt.*[63] In days gone by they used to call it abandonment to Providence: which wasn't all that stupid. Samuel Butler reconciles the two (*marvellously,* as if by chance) when he writes: *chance did as Providence willed . . .*

Saint Thomas or: *bête de somme* in five senses.[64]

Mania for justification: out of hatred (or fear) of the irrational.
    To justify the world, evil, the cops, bullshit, morality . . . It's an illness. The more so since all that is strictly *indefensible.* That is precisely why we have recourse to God: the demonstration gives the appearance of satisfying reason, and at the same time the incomprehensible-infinite silences it. Two birds with one stone: parade of humility and assurance of infallibility. Little matter to those explainers if, when the shameful secret's out, nothing is explained.

By a delectable and predictable conjuncture (for all thoughts come down to *the same thing*), the obsessions of the malcontents and the pessimists are exactly identical: they believe that everything *must* vindicate itself and are morally shocked at the setback.

I, who am not hampered by reason, feel no need to be "consoled" for the irrational and the absurd, which I find, on the contrary, very much to my taste and, above all, far more amusing.

■ Metaphysics of fun

For God, to be only God is really a bit much.

The degree of religiosity is, at least to begin with, in direct proportion to the development of the glutea maxima *muscles. It will be obvious, without further explanation, that women remain more devout than men.* (Alfred Jarry, *Speculations*.)

As a matter of certainty there exists a mysticism of poodle-clippers.[65]

There are imbeciles who believe that art is a serious matter.

Perfect beauty calls for admiration: it is deadly boring. Imperfect beauty must be, as it were, welcomed, won over and, so to speak, wheedled. The rift of irony is that redeeming imperfection.

We confuse *beautiful* with *big*, *slender* with *skinny*: a beautiful pig, a skinny leg.

■ Tacky poetics

The beautiful must be incongruous.

Beauty is an excess: not to be confused with perfection, which is only an average.

Genius manifests crudity. Neither Monsieur Raphael nor Monsieur Racine have it.

Avoid like the plague commercial travellers bringing cameos.

The majority of artists exhibit their ideas, new or newly turned inside-out, the way peasants do their Sunday clothes.

A botched garland[66] — that's the work of art. Just a little bit more finished and it would be quite perfect for getting itself garlanded. It was perhaps out of fear of garlands that Michelangelo was never able to finish anything. Colossal as his works were, he saw them still too much as garlands and sought some immoderation wherewith to botch them.

■ Uneasy going   He was so successful that he left everything *unfinished*. Never push things.

To foul things up in an elegant manner is not so much the art of aristocrats as that of poets. Poetry is knowing how to do things, even in the worst of bad taste, with *a good grace*. True of the poet, but also of the reader who must be on his guard, for fear of being a-poetic. There is no sad poetry.

I do not know, I suspect. (This is not a motto, it's an observation.)

It is easy to be original or to pass for such. I have had that reputation (to be such, and even, among some, of seeking to pass for such). However, if those *psychologists* could record the number of banalities that occur to me in twenty-four hours, they would regard me as a brother, and even an inferior brother.

The most insupportable hypocrisy — that of the aesthetes.

If they laugh, they hasten to save their laughter from frivolity by justification: Such a great comedian!

■ **Stick-in-the-craws**

The best jokes are *uncalled-for*.

Being able to laugh at one's own laughter and to make fun of the serious way in which people amuse themselves.

If it could be conscious, classical comedy would be perfect, so stupid is it (Molière's jokes). And those who laugh like a drain at it would (if they SUSPECTED) be the really DEAD-pan jokers.

Humour is scarcely more than a fairly revolting variety of the commonplace comedy. It is a position, a situation, almost a brand-name.

We are pretty well *beyond* those soft-boiled amusements.

Our business is with sniffed-out complicities and the open secret, laughter refused although affected and earnestness treacherously encouraged, the savouring of the pure spectacle of imbecility in its triumphal necessity . . .

Our distinguishing signs: fake wit, the apt response inaptly timed, the joke that falls flat, conniving gravity, the lame pun, subtly clumsy bad taste . . .

But, of course, these are only signs, winks. It is not a question of taking this second-degree hoax seriously, nor, above all, of making it a "comedy" — but of polishing it off too, *and so on* (as Achras used to say[67]). For there's no end to that little game. To the point of exhaustion (of the player and the game).

Alfred JARRY.

Those who do not find him amusing are right. His witticisms are feeble, his humour forced, and even schoolboyish when he openly takes the piss out of the audience, his would-be comedy is lugubrious. Hence his relative lack of success, which is moreover for him a victory, the one and only. Lack of success which mutates into failure (or victory which becomes triumphal) if we consider his supporters themselves and their delectable misinterpretations when they feel themselves obliged to laugh — or, a still more delectable misinterpretation, when they laugh spontaneously. Ah! He's conned them, *one and all.*

■ *Poubelle au bois dormant*[68]

The vanity and ridiculous pretentiousness of *ornament* (style, decoration, architecture . . .) confer upon it all its value. I care about ornament because everybody likes it, and that's the way to pay THEM back in their own coin.

A literally perfect style should conceal itself so completely behind what it expresses that it goes unnoticed. But that pure literature would be the negation: thus, all writers, despite their pretensions to perfection, are utterly illogical, which puts us in their debt for their "originality" and allows literature to exist in the form of the unspeakable mish-mash that defines it.

I have no time for this impure literature, or for pure literature. The pretentiousness of the first is ridiculous, in the latter the result is dreary. I therefore resign myself — cheerfully — to bad taste. So much the worse for aesthetes disconcerted by imprudence or impudence, so much the worse for the mugs for whom it is the done thing to put them off the scent (including Proust, eh? . . .).

Words sleep. Their silence sends one to sleep.

Man is an animal that blathers. I assess, without light-headedness, the extent of my humanity.

■ **Word-blaze**[69]

A man entirely aware of the ambiguity of things and of words ought *at least* to wind up fusing them entirely. Like the world, the word reflects from its thousand facets. The point is to place oneself at the centre of the dazzling spectacle, where the correspondences themselves no longer have any MEANINGS (one no longer senses them, they no longer have meaning, they no longer orientate). One loses the facet. And the contradiction shines forth, at once logical and ontological. Then, quite naturally, the thing coagulates into the sign and the word solidifies into matter, sonorous and tactile. The kabbalists were not far from this result. Mallarmé perhaps glimpsed it. And, before him, there was Nostradamus.

I have never understood the interest one could take in a description. In the century of the photo. And even in another.

To denounce, once and for all, the mania for celebration.
    It's the procedure for "uplifting" works. In it the exclamation is favourite. A great deal of fuss is made about stylistic devices. Among which the most putrid are the Epiphoneme, and Pretermission, to say nothing of Hypostasis and Prosopography, Invocation, Deprecation and Defecation. One refrains (and excuses others) from "looking into it." It's the most convenient of literary alibis. Practical and hard-wearing. The tone is that of *Les Nourritures terrestres*, of *Esther*,[70] or of

English novels. Insane tisanes.

■ Pathono-
mastic

True poetry is embarrassing. It is *suspicion* in every dimension of the term. The poet creates only in that rapid and almost shirked retouching of ham-fisted irony, of the unfinished sketch, the failure flippantly suffered. As soon as the floodgates are opened, it's the great sewage-disposal. This coarse facility pours itself out in discourse and descriptions. Celebration there and then becomes *fausse d'aisance.*[71] Rimbaud must have kicked himself at having turned out Victor Hugo, and perhaps if he fell silent . . . In Max Jacob we detect a latent celebration.

But there's a moral to this. Celebration calls for an unawareness in the patient, otherwise it's disappointing. Isn't the celebration of the mass, after everything that has been said about mystery, blood, death, just that?

Beloved and bland, images are the swedes of the poem.

Speech resembles its inventor, the breather of the word and author of the Babelic hoax: by a curious cacalogism it is at once the by-product and the raw material of transports in common: it can therefore *normally* be erected only in common places, songs of muck-spreading, or water-closets. As soon as one wishes to forget oneself, far from these cacathedrals and these close-stools in common-sense corner where our muganthropes re-hash the bliss of their mutual squitters, one senses the language becoming constipated while, alas, all the time remaining every bit as filthy. No more relief. The words gasp their last and stink of oral morality.

How then, to *express oneself*, since that word itself adopts the scato-

sociological gripes and consecrates it as the standard model of
delivery? How to avoid this caca-phony, since, we know this from the
experts, silence is still more fetidly eloquent than the voice? The cesspool of language needs once and for all to be emptied.

■ **Diagraphasias**

But we know that's impossible. One can still refuse to eat THEIR
shit: one won't avoid squelching about in it. *One can't get started.* So,
seeing that we are obliged to make use of this faecal language, let that
be to speak of the ignominy that demeans it. This is a last resort: but
with this *luxury* — of seeing our coprolalia denounced precisely by the
pastry cooks of ordure. For although reformers may have them ingest
the *instintestincts* of history, they will stick with their collective
evacuations, fleeing into their void and cherishing their ideal *cacagnes*,
crap-feasts. It's the intolerable colic: Flaubert, Barrès, Péguy, Romain
Rolland, Roger Martin du Gard.[72] Do you have any notion of all the
senses of the verb *to beshit*?

So there's no obvious remedy. As soon as one opens one's mouth to
speak, it stinks of the social. There's no use being canny and turning
nimbly aside, spitting words out sideways, installing flush-toilets in the
interstices of the sentences, lighting suffocating fires of unseasoned
timber at the foot of the page, creating draughts to crack the lamp-
glasses . . . that might be less revolting than Musset, France, Duhamel
and other lavatory stylists, but, after all, nightsoil-men, even perfumed . . .

Jarry's scatology is thus far more ontological than our beshitters
would credit. It's a known fact; the *Statue of Memnon* that sings at dawn
(let's be indulgent to that bard who has in his repertoire *The Song of the
Disembraining*) works nights as a barrel-toting nightsoil-man.

The poetry of the alexandrine is a piece of ladies' work for gentlemen.

■ **The saw-
queen**[73]

This explains the character of certain "poets," and of a good few "poetesses" (a word which gives a nice sound to the inadmissible).

Lyricism: a venereal disease.

But of course, but of course, it has to be said: La Fontaine, I won't drink your water.[74]

To shut poetry up in the poem is to prevent it penetrating into life. Let's not write anything any more. The poet of tomorrow will be unaware of the very name of poetry.

I knew a poet who got through his life — as one does a café-crème — turning out hundreds of self-obituaries. I knew another who wrote his poems pastry-cook fashion, with a funnel-shaped device and various sugars, pink, green, blue, mauve . . . And, when the poem was finished, he would eat it. Why not say that I take those two fellows, along with myself, for the three greatest living poets?

■ **Vagabond**

All the great endeavours — or, what comes to the same thing, every poetic endeavour — have been directed *against* language and thought.

To attempt to restore to thought the fundamental and *unthinkable* ambiguity which is nonetheless THE reality: to take language apart and *get out* of literature. Lautréamont, Rimbaud, Hölderlin, Mallarmé, Jarry, Fargue, Jacques Vaché . . . It's *impossible* anyway. First-degree failure.

But, on top of that, there's a second-degree failure. For, far more cruelly than the failure of their "career," the present or coming fame of those *horrible workers*, makes them FAILURES: although often without their knowledge, they are still at the origin of a literary form. Verlaine did not understand that it was *in that respect* that they were damned.[75]

It is no longer for us to start the experiment over again: that's clear enough. After Lautréamont, Rimbaud and Jarry, those who still write seriously are cunts (I'm moderating my language). The arts have exploded: there's no use in our taking poems for lanterns.[76] Let us render unto those arts what was due to those arts, and what is due to play, to play.

What I do is futile, not useful. No matter. I am neither a man of letters, nor a poet, I don't even claim to be interesting. I'm amusing myself. And I get up their noses, all of them. For me the admission of tragic silences is still over the top. It's not for me to admit anything. I do *nothing at all* —as I committed those verses — flippantly.

A poet who is preoccupied with poetry is a shopkeeper.

If a drunk spins you a yarn about faked poems, listen to him with all your heart.

■ **Tail-light**

With their eyes closed, today's Surrealists are drawing dud cheques on an inheritance misappropriated by the manoeuvres of legacy-hunters and mortgaged to the frontiers of nothingness. In their way of life as traders in the tarted-up tragic and brewers of small beers/biers without corpses, they have preferred the golden calf to the lean kine, problems to the poem, and the *faire savoir*, the tip-off, to *savoir faire*, know-how.

They know how, at the opportune moment, to whip out of their hip-pocket the testimonial-fruit-of-blackmail before which the doors of the bookshops fly open — or else the ultimatum written in antipathetic ink.

Their programme: to plant flags at every cross-roads of existence, to ensure that their past, from now on, takes the place of their future and exempts them from casting out the nines, to cry scandal if one asks them to show their pass by demonstrating they're not bone-idle. For the rest, to do sod-all with distinction. Hermit-crabs of poetry, infatuated with their monocled jelly-fish, here come Dada's boys.[77]

The literature of impotence is about to develop beyond measure.

Only repetitive twaddlers can still persist in "healthy" description and "optimistic" preaching, beatific clearance-sales of boredom.

■ Luna Park eclipse[78]

Thus we are on the point of seeing wholesale and retail nihilism, the psychological novel with (for profundity's sake) pessimistic resonances, philosophy in despair, Dostoyevski touched-up a little bit, and even various helpings-out for original sin . . . to say nothing of the (uncomfortably acknowledged or uncomfortably unacknowledged) postulates of Dada and others . . .

Unfortunately Lautréamont has passed this way. After the fearful purge he administered to humanity, all those little clysterical laxatives are pretty anodyne. In annihilating "good" literature, he has not neglected to render the other useless.

With the diabolical refinement of an apparent return to the arguments of reason (which once again lose their scanty meaning), his *Poésies* make short work of all the efforts of future "black" writers and the innocents who saw (and still see) in Maldoror a romantic pessimist. It's the fist that flattens would-be ingenuous uprightness! No more retreat. And no key to Lautréamont; for Lautréamont is not a door (not even an exit-door): when the house is blown up, there's nothing to shut or open.

It seems from now on that pessimism is only an attitude. Let's be cynical: there isn't even a question to pose. Only imbeciles or women are reduced to pondering about happiness. Laughable — and thereby, of some use.

One suspected as much: Voltaire didn't in the least understand Pangloss. *All is for the best in the best of all possible worlds* is the most vigorous and rigorous expression of absolute pessimism which, at this cusp, becomes radiant and takes up a position well *beyond* itself, saying to each event: "Why not? As well you as another."

As if there were lost time![80]

■ *Au petit malheur*[79]

The tragic: a stately name for ham-acting.

What do you reckon? Are we still to take the world for a philanthropic enterprise? As if something were owed us? By whom? There's still a bit of God hidden under that.

Botched consolation of presenting oneself as a spectacle to others and to oneself: destiny "is hounding" me. That would be too great an honour.

Pas d'histoires![81] Only histories are tragic. And we know perfectly well what use they are. Happy peoples do without. Histories are what get told (and, above all, get added to). But, noble as they might be, one does not live in sentences. And, bosses apart, they don't feed anybody.

For my part, I don't go for that bread.[82] I've even cottoned on there's no use changing the dough — it's always the *same* mush.

Malediction is only faulty pronunciation. If God — and a good few others after him — had taken lessons in diction, they would have avoided making fools of themselves. But it won't be me that'll regret it.

For all that, it's not a question of taking oneself for an enigma when one's only *crosswords*. No use setting out on a crusade only to find the solution (or dissolution) in the depths of a sepulchre.

■ **Nimis habens**[83]

To watch. To take shelter if there's a roof. But not to be so mistaken as to clap or hiss, *and to believe in it.* What fails is every bit as interesting as what *succeeds*.

BEWARE OF GAMBLING

"literally and in every sense." The beard of Saint Thomas More. Which I express as two equivalent postulates:
   1. *Everything is equal.*
   2. *Everything is thus perfectly good.*
   Only the gullible fool is surprised, only the simpleton finds fault. We have no right to anything, because there is no right, either in nature, other than that of eat or be eaten, or in society, where certain appearances mask the same reality. And there's nothing sad about this. On the contrary. Ordure? Now, there's a fine word for you. But isn't it fun, scrabbling around in dustbins? Poetic even. I'm speaking with a full knowledge of the facts.

Happiness? Of course, of course. It's with that they force people to make themselves unhappy. Me, I don't give a fuck.

For several centuries scientific stylishness has, more and more, proscribed the anthropocentric world, and we can be less and less astonished that this world should not be the land of Cockayne: *no longer even any need* to be victims of an original sin. Fortunately the hawkers of social progress have come on the scene to sell us perfect futures solely in order that we can, by comparison, whinge on indignantly to our hearts' content about the lack of concern as far as we are CONCERNED.

■ **When the caiman goes, anything goes**[84]

For the optimist everything's fine: all those disorders, stupidities and trivialities *are part of* the harmony. What a pessimist!

For the pessimist, everything should be far better: he seems to believe we could conceive of the universe *otherwise* than absurd, and mankind as *otherwise* than mediocre. What an optimist!

The evident satisfaction of pessimists in being such. There are likewise some who are positively beaming with delight at showing how their pessimism still isn't pessimistic enough.

Myself, just now, I illustrate the illusion of all thought — which eats its heart out with well-being. *Euphorisms.*

Despair is a business. With a bit of acumen it can be profitable. Every bit as much, on average, as the trade in hope.

For buying or selling, I haven't got a red cent.

■ *Le caniveau d'or*[85]

Is there still time? *There's always time:* time is always there, to take us out of ourselves. If only by that dreadful miracle of deliverance (even without the moment-to-moment expectation of the unforeseeable hurricane one hopes for to the end) the present is always the best, even when it is bad.

For me the best periods are the worst. Not because that would justify my pessimism and give me the opportunity to hate the Universe: it is common knowledge that I am always cheerful and, for all that, very sociable — thanks to my consummate experience of 'Pataphysics. But because, in those moments, *I stick at it.*

What is it the rat can do best, once it is in the cage? Eat the bacon. (Hebbel)

My greatest discovery has been to love my boredom and get fun out of it. I spent eleven years at school. And I realised there are no "sicknesses of the soul." There are only words.

■ The starch of time

Therefore I shall be serious, boring, cantankerous, miserable, deeply disappointed. I shall carry my head underneath my arm. Pay your respects to my stiff collar, pretty lady: it's from the Middle Ages. As for my head, it was Charlemagne's crown, and even more the truncheon-blows, that gave rise to the conflagration of the cobble-stones. You remember, dear hostess? You were so scared you got into my bed. I slipped behind the curtains. The green lizard followed me, "covered"[86] by the eyes of the dragoon, who, like the rest of his regiment, was making love to the housemaid.

Knowing that there is no future that is possible or desirable, I experience the solace one feels on going back to sleep when the alarm-clock has sounded.

There are still imbeciles who believe that *something will change.*

As if one wished to change bodies: one changes one's dress, wig, make-up, one's nose if need be . . .

One never changes anything but the flourishes, the frills; but the *text* remains the same. Only illiterates are taken in.

A curious species of illiterate: the learned specialists in frills. They have turned this knowledge into a science that is very complicated and often very boring (but what is there that does not interest us in the end?). They succeed in extracting from the frills a sort of law or system they call "progress" (history, social structure, political evolution, culture) and end up discovering a means — more or less imaginary, no matter — of working on the frills. They unleash cataclysms, wars, or revolutions accomplished at great expense, and everything else once again becomes more or less the same. In effect, whether the frills be maximalist or minimalist, legitimist or corporatist, French or Germanic, or whatever you want, they amplify a single text —THE text: those who command, command; those who obey, obey: and power is absolute. Only wait until our revolutionaries triumph: you'll see their police.

■ **Reason to let**[87]

We others, we have them on our backs.

Don't believe, though, that a change of frills would be completely pointless: for those who need a drug or something-to-live-by, it's still better than nothing.

It's only the idiots who are in the right, it's only weaklings who explain themselves, it's only the sick who have reasons for living.

For us life is a fact, no less, and, above all, no more.

The spectacle of encompassing stupidity is a stimulant that is by no means to be despised: it's as if bacillae secreted their own antitoxins.

Life would be dismal if it weren't for the ill-disposed. They season this dish of noodles.[88] I suspect that when Jesus said to his disciples: *You are the salt of the earth*, he had in mind those successors who would make it their business to piss-off the rest of humanity.

I don't know whether one should prefer performing dogs to mad dogs.

■ **THEIR wooden horses**

Every day they recite their "I"-lesson.

Faithful and a fawner, a sniffer and menial, thought turns *round and about* to make its bed and *earn*, O dream, the right to fall asleep. Candid and canine.

Whether it lies down on feathers or on straw, on hay or on old uniforms is of no great importance.

Atheist or not, revolutionary or not, worker or bourgeois, man of letters or boneheaded philistine, scientific or poetic — by more or less minute nuances (beauty of the crockery or elegance of the vocabulary: and still more!) — it's still the same life, and these seemingly contradictory ideas *serve* exactly the same *end*: getting shot of it and serving it. I admit that I've long since failed to distinguish between these distinguished-ones.

The *only* distinction would be between the yarn-spinners and those who don't spin yarns. But are there any?

And don't get the idea that there'd be any remedy there. There's no remedy because there's nothing to cure.

■ **The least that can be said of it**

"Making one's living"? By that THEY mean "earning (?) a living" all day long and keeping aside a couple of hours for dreaming about what it might be. The bedside mats slide under their bare feet as soon as they have their shoes on. Longing for travel, for painting the town red.

Just one more, to smash the glass of their aquarium? Not that stupid. Congratulations that keep them from forcing the locks. For them it's enough to remain voyeurs. Another way of holding on to their jobs.

THEY *"lend a hand."* With interest calculated on the product of the general interest and the rate of morality, divided by the sum of particular interests.

The word "detritus," with its melancholy, noble and latinate air, suits THEM to perfection.

All they will leave behind them is overflowing latrines. (Leonardo da Vinci)

That arse-cheek smile on THEIR faces? Remember the cosily senile euphoria those with head-wounds experience when the frontal circum-volutions are sufficiently penetrated.

■ **Comfit-box of crabs**

THEY become mad, but they remain boneheads.

Those newspapers I'm stupid enough to re-read.

Here we are in the century of *information*, that is to say the unformed. *Oncq plus d'horreur ne plus dire journaulx.* [*Never more horror nor the papers tell.* Nostradamus, Centurie II, quatrain 303.] All we have seen is as nothing compared to the cyclopean encyclopaedia of stupidity they are amassing with an ant-like tenacity.

Every kind of literature will be journalistic, with science for ballast. Paul Bourget[89] will be regarded as sprightly and dangerously whimsical. Everything will have a "mission." Every poem will be a slogan or advertising-copy. Novelists will be social-thinkers. By dint of sparing us from reading books, literary journals will come to replace them. Committees will decide on the form and content of productions to be undertaken. And, to have the right to practise, writers will have to be registered like prostitutes. Nobody will think of laughing at this farce. It will be suppression by seriousness.

I'm addressing myself to my fellows: *Watch out! Not a word! Police!* The journalist is an ideological cop.

■ *Le pince-homme*[90]

To kill in pursuit of theft is perfectly commonplace. To kill for killing's sake is to display a serious propensity to boredom. To kill out of absent-mindedness, routine, a concern for respectability, is fashionable. To kill for a laugh is the privilege of genius. But not to kill, that's where the drama begins.

In the facsimile reproduction of the great Atlantic manuscript of Leonardo da Vinci, we can see a *"tool for opening a prison from within"*: it's a kind of burglar's jemmy, extremely sophisticated, and which must in fact be very practical. *Is fecit . . .*[91]

> *The train cannot leave unless the doors are closed*
> *Do not hinder their closure*

We have been warned. And since, in an underhand way, they call us "poets," they have taken care to express themselves in verse.

Don't let yourself be looked in the eyes by a dairywoman; all the more so if she isn't a dairywoman.

■ **On the point of love**[92]

Love is an *affaire*, a transaction. We say: affairs of the heart. One can therefore be successful in them with a certain coldness. — "That's less agreeable." — It's still a question of exchange, according to a barely unavowed contract. And the Grand Passion, which manifests itself by its absolute character, "begrudges" what it gives. Once one has grasped this, it is fairly easy to take out an insurance on the absolute.

Love is essentially an *attempt to return*. Not to return to childhood, as I know not which hypochondriacal hairdressers' assistants whisper, but a return to the intra-uterine life, *the longing for which guides our slightest reflexes*. — Sodomy brings to the fore a similar state of mind, even though, on reflection, it unveils more original anatomical perspectives: it reveals a strange effort to insinuate oneself into the subterranean labyrinths in which the animalcular tumult bubbles and the vital impetus inflates. — On the one hand a quest for the melting sweetnesses of degustatory life: on the other hand, a quest for the dynamism of deflagrating life.

He told me: "You know, I'm getting married; it's to have kids. That way, when they're seventeen, I can sleep with them." Not a bad idea. But what patience.

■ Sourpuss

Shit in the basket, so as to put it on your head afterwards. (Montaigne, *Essays*, III, 5.)

We are so completely impregnated with egotism that to eat our own shit disgusts us, for all that, a little less than tasting that of others. Hence this test: would two persons so love one another that they would no longer make any distinction between themselves — would they unite to the point of faecal community? Eh, Marivaux?

MATERIA MATER.

Marriage is happiness in the *strict* sense.

An act of faith signed on stamped paper on the altar of jiggery-pokery, it mutually guarantees to the contracting parties the exclusive use of their respective sex-hormones, which thus find themselves *managed*: hence the term "*ménage*" given to that consortium, and which, by extension, is equally applicable to all the properties (in both senses of the word) of the two spouses; reciprocated violences do not escape this rule, but we no longer explicitly designate them by the doublet "*ménagerie*." The *strictness* of this legal instrument is plain to see. It is not even revocable for vice of chloroform.[93]

Cuckupiscences If homosexual practices had to "justify" themselves, it would doubtless be on grounds of disgust at that wet gut-rumbling heterosexual copulation.

Conjugal duties: coarse expression for what one fulfils. *Example*: the husband fulfils his conjugal duties. ENCYCL. We know that the primitives sanctify and adore the reproductive organs; the moderns have changed their appellations and passed from the religious vocabulary to Kantian terminology. This passage is called — who knows why? — progress.

His tie was fashioned from an umbilical cord.

Little children, watch out for Black Cat[94] condoms.

The only serious inconvenience of solitude is that when one has a parcel to wrap, one must at the same time press on the knot with one's index-finger and pull on both ends of the string. — But one manages by taking one end in the right hand and the other in one's teeth.

On the occasion of the erection of the Great Obelisk on the Place de la Fleur de Vigne, Onan pronounced a discourse on the exemplary dignity of Manual Labour. (La Bruyère, Characters, II.)

■ **Phallacious**

Which is the most obscene flower? The Ancients opted for the lily, on account of its donkey's member. I opt for the pine-flower

To write erotic novels, to be read in the dark. In Braillette.[95]

The perversions history attributes to Nero, Heliogabalus, the Marquis de Sade and Company, seem to me to denote only a perfectly decent puerility. Is that really all those men imagined in the art of sexuality?

Vice is there, simple and tranquil.

Woman is not the female of man. She represents a genus zoologically related to our own, but nevertheless dissimilar in its essence.
    It is high time to think and act in consequence.

What we call feminine charm is the g-string of claptrap.

■ **Don't come the muck**

A DISGRACEFUL INDIVIDUAL
    "Florence. — Alerted by the denunciations of several honest citizens, yesterday, the 8th of April [1476] the vice squad arrested one Leonardo da Vinci, aged 24, a painter, who indulged in unnatural practices on the person of the young Jacapo

Saltarelli, aged 17, a model, as well as three other individuals with certain tendencies. All these pleasant characters were taken into custody.

The trial will take place in two months before the Criminal Court of the City and the Public Prosecutor who, in accordance with the law, will demand the death penalty."

(THE NEWSPAPERS)

Above all never wear lily-of-the-valley in your flies; it brings too much good luck.

In knowing-not-what-they-do, THEY know all too perfectly well what they're doing

■ *Barre clouée*[96] There are only two *attitudes*: to resign oneself or to rebel. Both, if it comes to the crunch, demand the same liberty and the same lucidity. Unfortunately our rebels are still, and always, far too resigned, and our resigned-ones far too rebellious.

We underestimate resignation. Total, it could be most explosive. Epic. Nothing gets on top of the Resigned. Thus he is considerably more revolutionary than so many rebels. Piscator, the German communist theatre-producer, tells us how an amazing Czech writer, a scrounger and wanderer, has created an extraordinary type of "good soldier"[97] who, paying the most scrupulous respect to all the idols, unfailingly overturns them and — an admirable touch — without intending to or even noticing as much. In another category, the example of the Buddha. We do not sufficiently realise that force needs a point of application: THEY have need of obedience, but also of that minimum of resistance without which obedience is without its savour and command without triumph: a force is not deployed in a vacuum.

It is only imbeciles who win.

You reckon to save everything? — No, I'm not that ambitious: to save what can be saved. — If it were only a question of saving (and even saving everything), that would be too simple, you'd lose: but it's not even a question of that.

    You lose on account of not knowing how to lose. But you would gain nothing from learning it: for you would seek to lose in order to win, and since you would actually lose, you would have lost again and would not have been able to enjoy it.

The word "courage" provokes mistrust. But there is at least one sense in which I will not judge it to be pejorative, for God has no need of courage.

■ **Gagged at eleven o'clock**

What is repellent in the coward is that he blushes at his cowardice. It takes a great deal of courage to be truly cowardly.

From the caves to the barracks, from tetanising anxiety to a gross state of funk, man breathes in *fear* with oxygen. And when, modern-adult-and-free (without prejudice to fear of the police), he finds himself *emancipated*, he still pants to the same rhythm of death-rattle and death, after all, which we for that reason call "morality."

Morality is only a parody.

    By ascribing to remorse more real importance than to the act, it furnishes a virtuous pretext for disregarding the latter.

    What is more, the act itself, or at least what one might so

occasionally rediscover in it of liberty, of strength, of disinterest — is no more than the rough copy of the World of mutual glances and acts-in-common that are suddenly half-revealed and half-illuminated between supreme accomplices (or initiates) when, recognising one another, they at one accord abolish *all* morality.

■ *Lapsus à l'ami*[98]

There are two kinds of others.

One kind (these are the real others) are the hosts, the others (doubly other) are *outres*, leather bottles, those we disregard. Watch out! Let's not fill them with the wine we drink with our others, those frivolous barbarians who, without giving it a thought, share on the muddy quay the World's last crust of bread.

To say that the Uranist is *outside* of normal humanity — is that to reprove him to the extent that people suppose they do? Plato (by the creation of that term), and the Ancients, raised him *above*. In their days, in fact, it was understood that the law of the species affirms itself pretty well of its own accord and has no need of a *moral* halo. Christianity has changed everything by casting it thoughtlessly into the mire of concupiscence: since then the rights of nature have been the object of a long-drawn-out re-assertion, which we are still not done with, and which has had as its effect the setting up of instinct on a pedestal. The resistance to established morality has thus developed in accordance with a strict respect for genetic orthodoxy and, with a pleasurable convenience, non-conformity: rediscovering a beaten track as old as humanity itself, has been within anybody's means. In this way official immorality has joined with official morality in the condemnation of the Uranist; hence the baroque species of fanaticism we observe fuming as soon as we venture on to those shores. By way of a last word in the grotesque, the modern apologists for the Uranist imagine they need to cite references drawn from "nature," and link him with a deflected or poorly differentiated instinct. What would the Greeks have said about this absurd absolution? They would have despised it as apt only for cripples who neither Polycletes nor Praxiteles would have wished for models, and to whom their contemporaries would not even have paid any heed. Any more than Michelangelo or Shakespeare.

■ *En queue de poison*[99]

The example of the animals — that's all the moralists have to offer. And THEIR beloved *human dignity*? With that maxim one could condemn even THEIR progress. For all that, nature stands in need of being spruced up a bit. It has needed — all this, moreover, legally — to be decked out in sociological, psychological, diplomatic, jesuitical, selenic, or even india-rubbery trinkets, without which it would be too emetic. Rations of reason: fine for the guileless darlings and extra-pallid sweeties, lovers of regulations, over whom the police of the affections keep watch. For these conscripts in the bloom of youth, it is enough for them to catch sight of the gates of the maternal barracks from which they have emerged, for them to present arms. Bedridden banalities. I'm not particularly keen to give the last word to that "nature" which already contains within it the last of evils.

Apart from these serial desires, regulation affections, mawkishnesses with a touch of bleach-water, evaporating vapours and expectations of a Whore with a Heart of Gold, there are, for the curious and the hard--to-please, things *beyond*. More virile and rather unadorned. Perhaps less agreeable, certainly less sickly-sweet. Few, or no more, states-of-mind. An appeal that is no longer glandular birdlime or the tropisms of the crowd. That spark of toughness candour requires. That dulled twinge of intoxication liberty demands. Stupidity is still possible, to be sure, but less alluring. Above all, equality.

■ Equal and ego IT'S ALL THE SAME TO ME (I measure myself against it, and reckon myself its equal).

The inferior man accepts being inferior because he believes himself superior, or effectively is so in relation to others. When one treats him *as equal to equal*, he takes pleasure in this, because he thinks the superior is abasing himself, or that he is taken in, and thus inferior.

The majority above all love inferiority for its own sake, as a result of that deeply embedded taste for slavery which is one of the powerful sentiments of humanity, and which education makes its aim to develop beyond measure.

To be equal is more difficult.

He who poses the problem of honours is a shit. Either he despairs of attaining them, or he is looking for a way of accepting them.

Superior men or hierarchical superiors: I don't believe in superiors.

Equality ALONE.

Far less normal than superiority: to be confronted with an idiot. And yet, how much one resembles him!

■ Where everything comes together Nobody has ever given me orders. If some have reckoned to do so (in the army), I never noticed it. I have no need to have a world that's *in order*.

I have never given myself an order.

Everything I do will be too much.

What does it mean to "accept the human condition?" To accept is to take: when in fact it's we who are taken. To accept mankind, would that really mean recognising ourselves in the mirror? Yes — that's really us. So what, then? That's not to say we're not ugly.

Chance and the poet are alike. If they are creative, it is playfully, and their game of chance is the only true game. However, and although he works in a serious style, the so-called God doesn't do all that much better, and "his" works are scarcely distinguishable from their fortuitous crystallisations. Chance and the poet are *almost* as ham-fisted as he. I say *almost* because, all the same, he fails to be a good loser: he demands, when the chips are down, that we find everything he does perfect. For all that, ham-fistedness would be the *true* mark of divinity, were it not he who, according to common non-sense, was God.

To stake one's life at every instant, on every word, on every thought (for one has to think). And with one's eyes closed. It's straightforward affectation anyhow: the dice are loaded.

Not to be complete.

■ **The untamed pense-bête**[100]

Submerged by the flood, Jonah went right on pissing inside the whale.

What then was left to support you? — It was at this point that I discovered that I had no need to be supported by anything. Not even by the pride of not being supported by anything. I escaped even that heroism.

Throw the house out of the windows. (Castillian proverb)

We haven't got the Word.

    — Oh, but we have, we have; and I'm going to tell you it. *Or, then again, it's not worth the effort.*

    — ?

There you are, precisely! *That's* the Word.

The Last Word remains that of our friend Bosse-de-Nage, *Papio cynocephalus*.[101]

■ Dear ——[102]

   With your usual hypocrisy you are no doubt going to tax me again with hypocrisy. But I am firmly of the impression that I have told you all I know. The problem is that the only thing that interested the gentleman at the time was Prophylactophy. The gentleman wolfed down ideas. None of this is anything more than anecdotal, unworthy of an "intello." Things might be changing now. Imperceptibly perhaps, but we're getting there. And, Mother of us all, by canal, as Louté[103] used to say, we're going back to literature. So it's time to ogle the relics, as Julien would have said. In short, your hypocrisy is only matched by mine so I will not allow you to score points. In any case, to speak synthetically,[104] I shall concern myself with things passionately more interesting than yours, mine and J.'s hypocrisy united.

   I have no idea what became of him. I've repeatedly told you this. I only ever knew him for 3 weeks, the year of my *hypokhâgne*.[105] Afterwards, nothing. And everything else started to happen. Without any other rhetorical flourish. But, especially now, if I have long left behind me his *oeufs-aux-riz*, at the time, what with the literature of the Jesuits and of Pons,[106] it was a new world to me. One in which you make a late entrance, dear mammoth. I'm sure I've told you how it happened. The *how* was in some way more important for my education than the pohems themselves. Does the story give you a hard-on like some dirty old man? I'm sure you know it started at the public baths. I

■ **Witness:**
Letter from Philippe Merlen Concerning Julien Torma

□ Philippe Merlen (1915-1944). One of the circle of writers around Jean Giono, however all Merlen's MSS. were lost in the war. After a series of intense spiritual/ intellectual episodes Merlen moved from Trotskyism to Fascism and committed suicide while training for the Waffen SS.

had surreptitiously crept in from T——[107] where I was bored witless. Still hadn't stuck my face round the door back home and didn't know whether I would. The public baths were perfectly respectable. They were the only ones in Lille, as far as I know. A bit working-class, perhaps. I went into the first cubicle I saw. Inside there was a bloke without any clothes on taking off his socks. I said sorry and was about to make myself scarce, trying not to show any signs of embarrassment, which surprised even me. But as you know, everything that happened afterwards came as a permanent surprise to me! The bloke said to me "How do you like cold showers?" I replied, with my usual gift for quiet repartee, "Just fine." He: "Try this one." I thought it all rather funny (funny ha-ha). He said something along the lines of "I only like it if someone rubs me down." And he gestured for me to remove my clothes. All this almost in a whisper above the racket of icy water. It was too late to escape. In a flash, *in ictu oculi*, I was ready. Obviously, I realised that I was in for some rather special training for my paschal communion. But I wasn't in the least bit sorry I'd given grandma the slip. The bloke didn't have the look of a madman or a *littérateur*, more like working-class made good, not without a sort of discreet elegance, physically I mean, as far as one could tell at any rate. Anyway how could I judge? It all happened so quickly. We went into the shower. He made me stand behind him, my chest facing his back, and rub myself briskly against him while holding on to his shoulders. *And that was all.* Despite the cold, given that I was wearing nature's garb this did not fail to cause a certain intrinsic rigidity in the end. The age is unforgiving. But we quickly put our clothes on, without any further ado, and followed each other out. He explained to me the layout of the stalls (it was not difficult to avoid being noticed as this one was set back round a corner).

The only other thing he said was that he would be there tomorrow. I never found out whether he worked this trick on a regular basis. Not able or never thought of asking him.

So as to be sure of making our appointment, I went straight back home to sleep at T— and managed to escape my grandmother, who no longer knew whether she was coming or going, the next morning. It was Good Friday. Everything happened as before. Returned rue. J. G.[108] under a pretext to do with the church and saw him after that almost every day (except for Easter Sunday and the Monday) during the hols. Always exactly the same thing, except that I became entirely used to the intrinsic rigidity, despite the cold water. However "pure" I was and however interesting I found this exercise, I was not so green as not to feel a certain sense of let-down. I told him so. He shrugged his shoulders. About the only thing I knew about him at that time was his Christian name.

The first Monday of the new term I recall that we met up again after school. At my suggestion, he arranged to meet me in the evening. It was the first time we had talked. He seemed surprised to learn that I was still at school. I had no end of trouble making up a story and getting permission to go to the cinema. My sister came with me. I met up with him after giving her the slip. He was with a young girl, a blonde, their hair was exactly the same colour and her limpid eyes reminded me of his. The resemblance was striking and it was because of this that I've always paid attention to such details. What happened next was predictable. I learned the use of Vaseline (I'd only had the vaguest notions before). And then what? He wanted me to fuck him as he fucked her. I never found out if he liked the one without the other. Another thing, he couldn't bear the idea of me giving him a "hand job." Nor sucking him off. Not that I'd ever done it before. But I couldn't help asking if he would like me to suck him off after watching his "whore" (as he so gallantly referred to her) do it for him. Later I observed that he wouldn't let himself be kissed on the mouth.[109]

It was peculiar in the shower the next day. I thought that... And no, not at all. Nothing out of the ordinary. After what had happened though we started to talk about "matters of general interest," as the intellos say. He spoke to me of his books and gave me the ones that I showed you. I've still got them at Boulevard J——. We saw the girl again. Quite innocently as far as I was concerned. I hardly wanted to make an advance. He didn't suggest anything. I found it all very unsettling. It was good to be in love for the first time. The first time that really meant anything. And I shan't disguise the fact that I was smitten. He was more than delicate in his behaviour, and so perfectly at ease that he made you feel at ease too. He also disappointed me. I expected more. Without knowing exactly what. *As a sort of assurance,* without him having to do anything nor without noticeably having to beg him, I managed to get him to . . . Yes. It would be too much to say that it came as a revelation! But with him nothing could be displeasing. Basically, it seemed very . . . moral. I was naïve. He left Lille the next day. I never saw him again.

With that you have it all. Keep it in your file of compromising documents. For when I become a dictator. It will earn you a place in the Académie or worse if I can think of it.

You were right to find him a better sort of bloke. He's a thousand times better than you. But that means nothing. In your favour. *Sat prata.* The usual and the not so usual compliments. Yours,

Philippe

■ Jacques Vaché

☐ (All of the
photographs of
Vaché date from his
military service:
1915-18.)

■ The year before King Ubu first imposed his rotund presence on the French public, Jacques Vaché was born (1895). His family later moved to Nantes, not far from Alfred Jarry's own birthplace, Laval. As a young art student, Vaché had read much of Jarry's satirical and mystical writings and at times patterned himself on Jarry's stumbling and arrogant anti-hero, Ubu.[110] When the young André Breton met Vaché in 1916 at a Nantes hospital (where Vaché was being treated for a shrapnel wound), they shared this admiration. Breton, working as a medical intern during the war, wrote about Vaché's eccentric Ubu-like behaviour and love of costumes: "Sometimes he strolled the Nantes streets dressed in different uniforms: as a Hussar lieutenant, an aviator or a doctor. If he happened to walk by, he would ignore you completely and continue on his way without so much as a glance backward." [111]

Vaché was fascinated by costumes; Breton noted Vaché's drawings often resembled illustrations from fashion magazines, while his letters frequently refer to clothes in connection with action. Another of Vaché's "Ubuesque" gestures emerges in the oft-cited story of his interruption of the première of Guillaume Apollinaire's play *Les Mamelles de Tirésias*. Vaché, dressed as an English aviator, drew a loaded revolver and threatened to shoot up the theatre; surely one of the most extreme examples of theatre criticism to date. As a product of this new century, Vaché saw reality itself as a game; it was all a question of style. He often fantasised about major deceptions while he indulged in such pranks as introducing himself and others under false names,

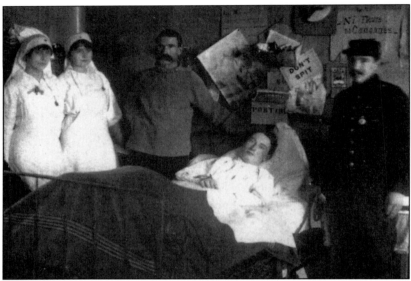

☐ Vaché wounded
in hospital.

wearing a variety of disguises, bragging about invented pasts, etc.
Vaché was also an Anglophile, sharing Arthur Cravan's admiration of
Britain and the United States. The war had revealed the hypocrisy of
an old world in confrontation as it tried desperately to cling to an
antiquated world order, what Vaché referred to as "nostalgic things
that died before the war — and then — what afterwards? We'll laugh,
yes?" Breton happily presented his individualistic new friend to
Théodore Fraenkel, an army doctor with a mordant wit who
participated in Dadaist activities, and his boyhood friend, Louis
Aragon. Breton also introduced Vaché to the works of a new
generation of writers, artists, and others of the French avant-garde,
although he later admitted that Vaché was not always taken by them.
Yet at Breton's urging, the two planned to collaborate on various
works: a play, a film, woodcuts and drawings to accompany Breton's
poetry, etc.

The Great War shaped a number of artists and movements. The Futurists ran off into noisy battle while the Dadaists found their boisterous voice in exile within the complaisant peace of neutral Switzerland. "Revolted by the butchery of the 1914 World War, we in Zurich devoted ourselves to the arts," Hans Arp wrote in *Dadaland*. "While the guns rumbled in the distance, we sang, painted, made collages and wrote poems with all our might. We were seeking an art based on fundamentals, to cure the madness of the age, and a new order of things that would restore the balance between heaven and hell. We had a dim premonition that power-mad gangsters would one day use art itself as a way of deadening men's minds." Wilfred Owen wrote tender ballads and harsh denunciations of the war while Raymond Radiguet dismissed it rather off-handedly as *les grands vacances*, utilising it as both impetus and backdrop for his novel *Le Diable au corps*. Jean Cocteau wrote the semi-autobiographical novel *Thomas l'imposteur*, in which he detailed some of his own wartime antics as an *imposteur* in the auxiliary medical corps, sporting a designer uniform.[112] Perhaps the best reflection to have emerged from this period is Erich Maria Remarque's *All Quiet on the Western Front*, based on his own experiences, which humanised war and gave a face to the cannon fodder, the common soldier who is young and shaken and thrown into conflicts he did not create. "Men will not understand us," Remarque wrote, "for the generation that grew up before us, though it had passed these years with us here, already had a home and a calling; now it will return to its old occupations, and the war will be forgotten — and the generation that has grown up after us will be strange to us and push us aside. We will be superfluous even to ourselves, we will grow older, a few will adapt themselves, some others will merely submit, and most will be bewildered."

Reading Vaché's letters and knowing his final decision underlines these feelings of being "superfluous" even to himself, the uninvolved soldier playing at war yet knowing little beyond it. Life itself becomes a game to be played, shaped by chaos, confusion, and carnage, leading to the unasked and unanswerable question "Why." His response was 'umour, a word he coined to describe his own removed attitude to life and a response to the future, one which also included suicide. It was an attitude that contrasts with Remarque's comments on wartime "good humour" that newspapers reported from the front. "It's all rot that they put in the newspapers," he wrote, "about the good humour of the troops, how they are arranging dances almost before they are out of the front line. We don't act like that because we are in good humour: We are in good humour because otherwise we would go to pieces."

Vaché detested patriotism in all its forms. Yet Breton himself labelled these missives as *War Letters*, and Vaché continually writes about this "playing at war," a game that allows him to dress up in uniforms within roles delineated by military ranks: the soldier, the aviator, the translator, the opportunity to mix with British and American troops for his own amusement, and the tweaking the noses of officers and officials. "Several times I've told a colonel to whom I'm attached that I'll push a bit of wood into his earens[113]," he wrote. "I doubt that he quite understood me wholly . . ." Or later: "I was introduced today to a Division General under the name of a famous painter . . . They (the General and Staff) managed to run away from me as soon as possible." He is entirely unable to suppress the scoff.

Although frequently written about, biographical information on Jacques Vaché is sketchy. Born in Lorient and the youngest of four children, he was the son of a marine artillery captain and spent his early years living in Indochina. When Vaché's father quit the service in

1912, the family moved to Nantes, where young Jacques teamed up with three friends at his lycée — Jean Bellemère (who later wrote under the pseudonym Jean Sarment), Pierre Bissérié, and Eugène Hublet — to put out several literary reviews. In 1913, Vaché enrolled in the École des Beaux-Arts under the painter Luc-Olivier, ending his studies when he was drafted the following year. After his spell in the hospital for a grenade wound, Vaché returned to the front as an interpreter for the British troops. These facts are cursory. Vaché is most remembered for his suicide, a final "'umoristic" or "ubique" act, in which he was accompanied by one of his "unwitting" Army buddies. It will never be known if this double suicide was intentional or whether Vaché's drug overdose on the evening of 6 January 1919, was merely a tragic accident.

Suicide was viewed as a logical option for those in the French avant-garde and appeared repeatedly in the poetry of Louis Aragon. Vaché's letters broach the subject several times in an off-hand accepting manner; and, apart from Rigaut and Cravan, the subject of suicide was also a regular theme in the works of René Crevel, who killed himself on 18 June 1935. Vaché died of an opium overdose and, though the Dadaists and Surrealists weren't known for their drug habits, opium certainly abounded in French artistic circles. Both Cocteau and Crevel were addicts and it had a considerable influence on their writing. Drugs could create distorted states of consciousness, although the Surrealists themselves opted to achieve these states without chemical or organic aid. Vaché's ease in writing about drugs in his second letter to Breton demonstrates that this habit was not such shocking or bizarre behaviour.

After his death, Breton published these fifteen letters in three consecutive copies of *Littérature*,[114] later collecting them into a slim

volume published in August 1919 in Au Sans Pareil's *Collection de Littérature* series.[115] Breton referred often to Vaché's early influence and over the years he wrote various tributes to him, beginning with an oblique introduction to the first edition of these letters. Among Breton's writings is the following eulogy, in which he delivers perhaps Vaché's most poignant epitaph:

A young man of twenty-three, who scanned the universe with the most beautiful gaze I have ever known, has mysteriously departed from us. It is easy for a critic to say that this was the result of boredom. Jacques Vaché was not the man to leave a testament behind him. I can still see him smiling as he spoke the words 'last will.' We are not pessimists. This man, who was painted lying on a chaise-longue, so very fin-de-siècle, to avoid disturbing the psychologists' categories, was the least disturbed, the most subtle of us all. I can still sometimes see him as he was when he explained to a provincial fellow-passenger in a tram: Boulevard Saint Michel — Quartier Latin — the shop window signals its comprehension.

We are reproached with failing to admit that Jacques Vaché did not create anything. He always pushed the work of art to one side — the ball and chain that hold the soul back even after death. At the same time as Tristan Tzara was issuing his decisive proclamations in Zurich, Jacques Vaché quite independently confirmed Tzara's principal thesis: philosophy is the question whether we should look at life from the standpoint of God, the Idea, or from that of other phenomena. All that we look at is false. I do not think that the nature of the finished product is more important than the choice between cake and cherries for dessert.

Finally, a note on the translation. Vaché's punctuation in these letters is indeed singular and arbitrary. They were scribbled down hastily at the front and, of course, Vaché never anticipated their eventual publication.

Rather than clean up the punctuation and adapt it to more conventional English, I have tried when possible to retain Vaché's own peculiar use of dashes (often used arbitrarily in the place of a comma or full stop), capitalisation, parentheses, ellipses, etc.

In regard to Vaché's frequent use of the future verb tense in place of the conditional, and his many spelling errors, these have been corrected since they tend to distract rather than allow the reader access to Vaché's thought processes. A few of the most notable mistakes have been pointed out in the footnotes, and his frequent use of English words or phrases has been italicised.

□ Self-portrait as
an officer.

■ La Rochefoucauld — 27. ? 1916
13, rue des Tanneurs

Dear friend,

I've succeeded — not without some pain — in obtaining a pass from a small self-important and bristling major — and have finally arrived — after wagon wheels and icy train compartments — here — in this classic and obsolete hole — such as academics might describe when they dabble in "studies of customs." I arrived only last night — but I'm already convinced that the cashier at the tobacco shop is both fat and brunette — because of the non-commissioned officers — and that the café is called *"Du Commerce"* — because that's how it should be — Finally here, at least I'm free and feel somewhat at home.

What a hole — what a hole — what a hole! It always astounds me, if only for a moment, that there are people who . . . actually live here — their entire lives — So! — They're also "healthy people" — "old buggers . . ." — "who understand nothing about nothing" — Heap of poor devils who are gloomily humoristic — with digestive systems and bellies — My brothers — *"Noun di Dio!"*[116]

Ah! Ah! as Doctor Faustroll's Hydrocephalus might add. [117]

Well, I'm home.

I'd appreciate it — my dear friend — if you write me a few lines — But I should warn you that I'll be leaving this address next Sunday.

Say hello to my neighbour the stone-mason — and also to the citizens of Poland. [118]

I shake your hand.

J.T.H.[119]

P.S. — I noticed during the trip — in passing — that Saintes — is not in the Midi, next to the île d'Hyères, as I had thought — Let me tell you — travel broadens the mind.

**■ Letter Two
To André Breton**

■ X. 5 July 1916

Dear friend,

I've suddenly disappeared from Nantes' circles and so you must excuse me — But, M. Minister of War (as they say) — has found my presence indispensable at the front, at least for a little while . . . and I had no other choice.

I've been working in the capacity of interpreter for the British troops — A situation that is sufficiently acceptable in these times of war: being treated as an officer — horse, miscellaneous baggage and even an orderly — I'm even beginning to smell British (shoe polish, tea, and blond tobacco).

But all the same, all the same, what a life! I've (naturally) no one to talk to, no books to read, and no time to paint — in short, I'm *horribly* isolated — *I say, Mr. Interpreter — will you . . . Excuse me, the road to? Have a cigar, sir?* — Provisions trains, inhabitants, a mayor, and billeting paper — A shell that announces itself, and rain, rain, rain, rain — rain —

rain — two hundred convoy trucks in a line, in a line — in a line . . .

Over all, once again a *horrible* boredom has descended on me (see above); I am bored by uninteresting things — And for fun — I imagine that the English are in reality the Germans and that I am with them, and for them, at the front — Certainly I smoke a little "dope."[120] This officer, "in the service of His Majesty," is going to transform himself into a winged androgyne and dance the waltz of the vampires — while drinking tea with milk — and then I'm going to wake up in a familiar bed and go and unload the boats — with you beside me — brandishing an electric torch . . .

Oh! enough — enough! and even too much! — a black suit, creased pants, polished shoes — Paris — striped cloth — pyjamas and uncut books — Where are you going this evening? . . . nostalgic things that died before the war — and then — what afterwards?? We'll laugh, yes?

" . . . We'll go to town . . ."

"Your soul is a choice landscape . . ."

"His riding coat had the habit of bulging at the pockets . . ."

"With a happy heart, I went upstairs . . ."

The afternoon of the faun[121] and Caesaress . . . Elvira with lowered eyes and Narcissus' naked sister.

Oh! enough! enough! and even too much!

Sidney, Melbourne — Vienna — New York and back again — Hotel lobbies — varnished steamers, luggage ticket, Hotel Manager — phonies — and Return.

You see — I'm bored, dear friend — but I'm also boring you, and after some reflection, I think I should stop here.

Remember that I like you a lot (and you must believe this) — and that I would kill you moreover — (without scruples, perhaps) — after first having rifled you of unlikely possibilities . . .

Seriously, I now ask you to write to me . . .

Mr. Vaché — interpreter —

H.Q. 517th Div. Train A.S.C. B.E.F.[122]

I salute the citizens of Poland with all accorded formalities and ask that you remember me. All my best.

J.T.H.

P.S. I reread this letter and in short, found it — incoherent — and very badly written — I politely beg your pardon.

Dont acte.[123]

J.T.H.

<table>
<tr><td>■ Letter Three
To André Breton</td><td>■ X. 11 October 16
3 p.m.</td></tr>
</table>

Dear friend,

I'm writing to you from bed where an annoying temperature and delirium have me stretched out flat in the middle of the day.

Yesterday I received your letter — And it's obvious I've forgotten nothing of our friendship which, I hope, will endure — so rare are the sârs and mimes![124] Even though you only approximately grasp what I meant by 'umour.

I'm the English interpreter, a position to which I bring a total indifference decorated with a quiet farce — such as I like to bring to official things — I take my Crystal monocle[125] and a theory for troubling paintings for a walk around villages in ruins.

I've been successively a crowned man of letters, a well-known pornographic artist, and a scandalous cubist painter — Now, I stay at home and leave the task of explaining and discussing my personality to others.

The consequences don't matter.

And furthermore, I imagine I'm in the German Army and I've succeeded — Things change, now I truly believe I serve against the allied armies — What do you expect? . . .

I'm going on leave around the end of this month and I plan to spend some time in Paris — And I have to see my very best friend there, of whom I've completely lost sight.

A future letter from me will contain — and don't you doubt it — an effigy to war — all according to a post-criptum carefully crossed out.[126]

Where is T.F.[127] — I've written to the citizens of Poland once, I think, in response to two of his amusing letters.

Can I beg a response from you also? — I suppose — having once taken up the pen, that — in the future I will be able to use it more easily; besides, I've written to you once already, if I remember correctly?

Aside from that — which is trivial, of course — Nothing. The British Army, as preferable as it is to the French, is without a lot of 'umour.

Several times I've told a colonel to whom I'm attached that I'll push a bit of wood into his earens — I doubt that he quite understood me wholly — since he doesn't understand French.

My current dream is to wear a red shirt, a red silk handkerchief, and high boots — and be a member of a Chinese society without purpose or secret in Australia — Besides, I don't deny that there is vampirism there.

Have any of your enlightened ones the right to write? — I would gladly respond to anyone who's persecuted, or even to any "catatonic" whatsoever.

Meanwhile, I reread St. Augustine (I can just picture the citizens of Poland smiling), and I try to conjure up something other than a monk who has absolutely no concept of 'umour whatsoever.

Dear friend, I'm now awaiting a response . . . to this incoherence which is hardly worth one, and I ask you to believe in my memory.

J.T.H.

■ X. 29 - 4 - 17.

Dear friend,

At last, your letter.

There's no point — is there? — in assuring you that your presence often remains on the screen[128] — You sent me a "flattering" missive — No doubt to provoke some sort of response from me that a great comatose apathy always seems to put off — For just how long, as they say? . . .

I'm writing to you from an ex-village, a very narrow pigsty hung with blankets — I'm with the English soldiers — They have advanced quite a bit towards the enemy line near here — It's very noisy — And that's that.

My dear friend, I was happy to hear that you are sick, only slightly — I received an almost normal letter from T.F. — that boy saddens me — I'm tired of mediocrity and am of a mind simply to go to sleep for an indefinite period — For me, to go through the waking effort of writing these few pages alone is extremely difficult; perhaps it'll be better next time. Sorry — okay? okay? Nothing kills a man so much as having to serve his country — Also.

From time to time — and so I won't be suspected of a peaceful death after all, I assure myself through a trick or a hamicable[129] pat on some head of familiar death that I am a villainous man — I was introduced today to a Division general and a Staff major at headquarters under the name of a famous painter — (I think the said general was 50 or 70 years old — perhaps he is dead also — but the name remains) — They (the General and the Staff major) managed to run away from me as soon as possible — it's strange and I amuse

myself by imagining how unamusing this will end up — In any case . . .
Besides . . . And in the end it leaves me indifferent as to how it will all
turn out — it's not really funny — not funny at all. No.

Are you sure that Apollinaire is still alive or that Rimbaud even
existed? For me, I don't think so — I only see Jarry (Anyway, what do
you want, anyway — . . . — UBU) — I'm sure that MARIE
LAURENÇIN[130] is still alive: certain evidence exists that seems to prove
this — Is this right? — nevertheless, I think I hate her — yes — there,
tonight I hate her. What do you want?

And then you ask me to define 'umour for you — just like that! —

IT IS IN THE ESSENCE OF SYMBOLS TO BE SYMBOLIC

it seemed to me for a long time that the only thing that deserved to
exist was that which was capable of containing a horde of living things:
EXAMPLE: you know the horrible life of the alarm clock — it's a
monster that has always frightened me because of the number of
things its eyes project, and the way in which this honest man stares at
me whenever I enter a room — why then does he have so much
'umour, why? But then: it's thus and not otherwise — There is a lot of
wonderful UBIQUE[131] in 'umour also — as you will see — But — of
course, this isn't definitive and 'umour derives too much from a
sensation of not being very difficult to express — I think that it's a
sensation — I was going to say SENSE — also — of the theatrical (and
joyless) futility of everything.

WHEN YOU KNOW

And then, this is why enthusiasms (in the first place they are so
noisy) — expressed by *others* are so hateful — Because — isn't this
right? — We have Genius — since we understand 'umour — And

therefore, everything — Besides, have you ever doubted it? — is permitted to us — And besides, all this is very boring.

I'm sending along this fellow[132] — and I want to title it OBSESSION — or else — yes — BATTLE OF THE SOMME AND THE REST — yes.

He's been following me around for a long time and contemplated me innumerable times in unnamable holes — I think he tries to confuse me a bit — Thus, I've got a lot of affection for him, among other things.

J.T.H.

Tell the citizens of Poland that I want to write to him — and, above all, that he doesn't just take off like that without leaving a forwarding address.

It's boring to write with a pencil on lined paper.

■ X. 29. 4. 17

Dear friend,

I was happy to receive some news from you — And, even more, after all — to hear that you are in shelter — I'm bored a lot behind my glass monocle, I dress in khaki and fight the Germans — The disembraining machine[133] functions with a lot of noise; and not far away I have a stable for TANKS — very UBIQUE animals, but joyless.

I wrote to Reverdy[134] for a copy of NORD-SUD — perhaps it's not a hoax — I'd like you to send me some prints or drawings and other types of linear works. I dare to hope that you will take pity on one

□ Letter Five: picture captions. Top: *My sister the family whore.* Left: *My sister the village cow.* Bottom: *Troop morale.*

J'ai écrit a Reverdy
ou NORD SUD
- peut être n'est-ce
pas une mystification.
- J'adorerai à
que vous
m'envoyassiez
montrant
dessins et ces sortes de
procédés linéaires - J'ose
espérer que vous
pitié du qui est volé -
dans une nation étrangère à
guerroyer : et puis ce général
Pau qui n'est pas mort encor.
tout de même ! tout de même !
- En attendant une lettre
je vous salue en divers démiurges
Jacques Vaché

mon soul... des ... illes

mon frère Zosime le Panopolitain

□ Letter Five verso:
picture captions.
Top left: *My brother
the big city pimp.* Right:
*My brother Zosimos the
Panopolitan.*[135]

who is isolated in a foreign country waging war — and then that General Pau[136] is not dead yet — Anyway! Anyway!

— I'm waiting for an answer and I salute you and your various demiurges.

Jacques Tristan Hylar

■ **Letter Six**
To André Breton

■ 4. 6. 17

Dear friend,

I hope I'll be able to see you on my upcoming visit to Paris — (around the 15th or 16th) — I've also relayed this information to the citizens of Poland, in case the unreliable post office should lose one of these letters — Will you let me know if you'll be in Paris at that time?

It's burning hot here, very dusty and sweaty — but what do you expect? It has to be like this on purpose — The swaggering lines of large convoys stir up the dust and salt the sun with acid — How funny it all is! — Apollinaire — too bad! — Magazines frosted with blonde girls and the tough-guy detective's shaved nostrils are quite beautiful . . . *"The girl I love is on a magazine cover"* — Tough luck! Tough luck! — So what, that's how it is — Nevertheless, the white lilac flowers in the shell-casing that sweat and fall back into old solitary sensual pleasures bore me a lot — the summer sidewalk florists whose sprinkling hoses ruin everyone's good Sunday clothes — It's pleasantly warm and persons holding *lorgnettes* discuss, I think, the stock-market with the attitude of housewives — All the same again, very little of the smell of these old scraped melons and sewers escapes me! . . . — And then this young whore hanging up her underwear and her damp odour — ! — A fat green fly is swimming in my tea, its wings spread out flat — Oh well, too bad —that's all — *Well.*

— *Well* — I'm waiting for a letter from you, that is if you care to write. Meanwhile, the banal buzzing of aeroplanes glorify themselves with white tufts of powder; and I hope this horrible bird spins straight into the blinding brilliance while pissing a thread of vinegar.

Your friend,

J.T.H.

P.S. Enclosed is a letter owed to the citizens of Poland, since I can't find the address anyway.

■ 4. 6. 17

■ Letter Seven To Théodore Fraenkel

I have just this very instant received your *Practitioner's Journal* for which, dear colleague, I must thank you — Tough luck . . . ! Have all the collaborators at SIC ganged up to pull Mr. Le Birot's leg?[137]

You know, the war isn't over yet — and this morning the Germans again sent us a volley of bullets, though 12 kilometres from the line — It would be annoying to die so younggggg.

Ah! then PSHIT.[138]

I'm leaving here and my boredom will take me to see you in Paris — Because I hope to find your presence there around the 15th or the 20th of this month. Write me a short note and tell me you'll be there, if you so deign — and also, try to arrange some sort of spectacular

□ Letter Seven,
picture captions.
Top left: *Moral
Anguish*. Top right:
*Type of Death for the
Country (acquired by
THE STATE)*. Bottom:
*Another Type of Death
for the Country
Acquired by THE
STATE)*

et puis les mauvaises plaisanteries
me font fusiller quelquefois —

— Pourtant je compte vous
voir — j'attend un mot ?—

votre très devoué

Auguste Hydar.

event to great effect so that together we might be able to kill some people before I have to leave — Since mail takes an average of six or seven days to reach me, write me as soon as you receive this letter.

Did I tell you I received "LES CAVES . . . "[139] and "THE POET"[140] — Apollinaire — he's still amusing sometimes — he must need some Phynance,[141] all the same — GIDE — Oh well — Gide — it's fortunate he did not live as THE ROMANTIC — I think what a sad Musset he would have made — He's nearly cold already, isn't he? In any case I thank you for sending me these books — I really could no longer read "ALLAN MASON – DETECTIVE" or "THE INN OF THE GUARDIAN ANGEL"[142] and then all the bad jokes shoot me sometimes.

However, I expect to see you soon — and I'm waiting for your answer.

Devotedly yours,

J.T.H.

■ **Letter Eight**
To André Breton

■ X. 16. 6. 17

My dear friend,

I received your note last night. I'm now taking the liberty to include in this sort of letter a sort of drawing. Because, frankly, I can now only paint with coloured ink.

As I announced to Mr. J. Cocteau[143], I'm happy that I'll be seeing you very soon, assuming of course, that I'll be allowed to go to Paris on the afternoon of the 23rd. And so, I could very well go to see *Les*

Mamelles de Tirésias, by Guillaume A.[144] — about whom — and this is another Story — I'll hold my judgement this afternoon — Have I told you that I find Gide truly cold?

The third beginning to this note — THIS IS BEGINNING TO IRRITATE ME — Apparitions of broken puppets that ramble on and on or else delight you! I kill the fourth beginning. *Well.*

Did you recently receive, around a month ago, I think — a smiling individual, very nerve-racking, surrounded by faces[145], who many times — in anger — made me burst out laughing? — I think he dominated quite a few of my warlike escapades and I admit I would be disappointed if he were lost in the post — Well — now the stump — my pencil — it shortens and breaks — And then there is a heat that is full of flies and odours from half-opened food tins.

I remain your obedient servant.

J.T.H.

■ X. 16. 6. 17

■ **Letter Nine**
To Théodore.
Fraenkel

It's very hot, my friend, but I'll answer your letter anyway. You were very kind to have brightened me with radiance, and I hope in Paris — (of course, my leave was late) for Guillaume Apollinaire's Surrealist performance[146], which I suspect will begin a little late, perhaps.

Did you pay for the two franc's worth of gold braid that so dashingly decorates your uniform — or — (everything is possible, after all) — was this a gift from the State? And when are you going to bring order to your realm? — In any case, I hope to see you on my visit — ? My God, it's hot — I will never be able to win all these wars!!!

I'll probably arrive in Paris on the afternoon of the 23rd — Will you be in an aperitif for the "Rotonde"[147] around 6:30 p.m. — or, please tell me now if you even wish to receive this mish-mash at all, and tell me where, with a little luck, I may hook up with either you or the "Pohete"[148] — or even both of you at the same time? But don't plot an unpleasant encounter — I'm joking — of course it'll be fun — but please think about my visit to La ville-LUMIER (sic), even if only for a moment? — I'll be arriving — at the Quai d'Orsay — coming from A . . . around 4:30 . . . 6 p.m. — the afternoon of the 23rd.

Devotedly yours.

J.T.H.

**■ Letter Ten
To André Breton**

■ 18. 8. 17

Dear friend,

I've often thought about writing to you since your letter of July 23rd — but never decided on a definite form of expression — and I still haven't — Instead, I think it's better just to write an immediate improvisation at random — on a somewhat familiar text, one that is even slightly scripted. We'll see about producing something when the chances of our conversation have led us to a series of axioms adopted in common "'umour" (pronounced: *umoureau*, because, all the same,

humoristic!). In short, your idea about writing a play suits me[149] —
Don't you think it would be good to include (I don't insist on this at
the moment) — an intermediary character, somewhat between the
customs officer and your "modern" No. I — a sort of *avant-guerre*
tapir, lacking charm and not completely shaken off a lot of
miscellaneous superstitions, while in fact, he's already a confirmed
egomaniac — a kind of slightly surprised greedy barbarian — At any
rate . . . And then the whole TONE of our gesture remains to be
decided — I would prefer it to be dry, without literature and, above
all, not "ART."

Besides,

ART doesn't exist, of course — Then it's useless to sing about it —
nevertheless! We make art — because that's how it is and not
otherwise — *Well* — what are you going to do about it?

Then we neither like ART nor artists (down with Apollinaire!). AND
how RIGHT TOGRATH IS TO ASSASSINATE THE POET![150] — However,
since this is so, it's necessary to swallow a drop of acid or old lyricism,
doing it in a lively jerk — because locomotives go fast.

Modernity is also both constant and murdered each night — We
ignore MALLARMÉ, without hatred — but then he's dead
— But we don't recognize Apollinaire any more, or Cocteau —
because — we suspect them of making art too consciously, of slicing
romanticism with telephone wire and not knowing the dynamos. THE
Stars are still disconnected! — it's boring — and then sometimes they
speak so seriously! A man who believes is a curiosity.

BUT SINCE SOME PEOPLE ARE NATURAL HAMS . . . .

Ah well — I see two ways of letting things flow — To construct personal sensation by using a flashy collision of rare words — ones not often used — or draw angles, neat squares of feelings — naturally, those of the moment — We will allow logical Honesty — provided it contradicts us — like everyone else.

— O ABSURD GOD! — because everything is contradiction — isn't it? — and will 'umour be the one who is never taken in by the hidden and sneaky life of everything? — O My alarm clock — eyes — and hypocrite — who detests me so much! . . . and will 'umour be the one who will feel the lamentable optical illusion of universal simile-symbols.

— It's in their nature to be symbolic.

— 'Umour shouldn't produce — But what to do about it? I grant LAFCADIO[151] a little 'umour — because he doesn't read and he produces only through amusing experiences — such as the murder — and without any satanic lyricism — my old rotten Baudelaire!!! We needed our art a little dry; machinery — presses with stinking oil — hum — hum — hum . . . hiss! — Reverdy — amusing the pohete and boredom in prose, Max Jacob, the old fraud — PUPPETS — PUPPETS — PUPPETS — do you want beautiful puppets of painted wood? Two flame-dead eyes and the crystal circle of a monocle — with an octopus-like typewriter — I would like that better.

— This all bothers you a lot sometimes — but answer me — I'll be passing through Paris around the beginning of October and perhaps we can arrange a preface/discussion paper — What wonderful noise! — In any case, I hope to see you very much.

Accept my best wishes.

J.T.H.

■ 9. 5. 18.

Dear friend,

— It's true — according to the calendar — that a long time has passed since I have shown you any signs of life — I understand Time badly, all things considered — I think of you frequently — one of the very few — who willingly tolerates me (Besides, I suspect even you of a little mystification) — *Thanks.*

— My multiple meanderings — I'm vaguely conscious of storing up all sorts of things — or of rotting a little.

WHAT'S GOING TO COME OF THIS, GOOD GOD.

— For instance, I can no longer be a grocer — the attempt wasn't very successful. I then tried something else — (have I tried? — or have I been tried . . .) — I can hardly write about it now — We amuse ourselves as best we can — So there.

I am decidedly very far from the literary crowd — even from Rimbaud, I'm afraid, dear friend — ART IS STUPIDITY[152] — Almost nothing is stupid — art must be funny and a little tiresome — that's all — Max Jacob — very rarely — could be 'UMOROUS — but he also ended up taking himself seriously, didn't he? A curious intoxication — And then — to produce? — "to aim so purposely to miss your mark" — naturally, written irony is unbearable — but naturally you also know very well that 'umour isn't irony, naturally — *Like that* — what do you want? It's like that and not otherwise — Everything is so funny, very funny, it's a fact — Everything is so funny! — (and if we killed ourselves also, instead of merely going away?)

— *Soifs de l'Ouest*[153] — several passages made me rub my hands together — perhaps — better still if a little shorter? — André Derain[154], of course — I don't understand . . . "the first-born is the angel" — Besides, it's to the point — a lot more to the point than a number of things to be seen at the Nantes Hospital.

Your synthetic critique is very engaging — even more, very dangerous; Max Jacob, Gris escape me a little.

— Excuse me — my dear Breton, for the lack of making a point of all this. I'm in rather bad health, live in a hole that's lost somewhere between calcinated tree stumps and, periodically, a sort of parabolic shell dawdles by and coughs — I live with an American officer, who is learning war, chews "gum" and sometimes makes me laugh — I've escaped him very little since — to this last retreat — But I object to being killed in wartime — I spend the largest part of my days walking to the unlikeliest places where I can see fantastic explosions — and when I am behind the lines, often in the public house where I love to eat dinner — It's sufficiently lamentable — but what to do about it?

— No — thanks — dear friend, a lot — I have nothing ready at the moment — NORD-SUD — would they take something about this sad Apollinaire? — whom I don't dispute has a certain talent — and who had succeeded, I believe — in something — but talented he is — he writes very good "narratives" (do you remember the college?) — sometimes.

And T.F.? Thank him, when you write — for his numerous letters so full of funny observations and good sense — Well.

Your friend.

J.T.H.

■ 12. 8. 18.

Dear friend,

— I wanted to answer your long ago letter personally with a visit; but, naturally, you took the chance to get away — I'm almost always in prison for the moment; it's cooler there during the summer — nevertheless, I've some funny murders to tell you about — But then . . .

— I dream about some good well-felt Eccentricities, or some amusing deception that would result in lots of deaths, everything performed while wearing very light athletic-style form-fitting costumes, you know, with wonderful open-topped canvas shoes.

— But, I must offer no resistance — I'm confined to barracks here — in expectation of what new adventures? — Of course, all provided that they don't kill me while they have me here? . . . poor people . . .

— I hope this document reaches you while you are still alive and doubtless keeping busy cutting off arms and legs with a saw, according to tradition, and wearing a pale white apron on which a hand leaves greasy prints in blood.

— It seems to me that I am well, despite the fact I only understand such matters a little — but I don't spit — thanks — nor do I cough?[155]

J.T.H.

■ July-August 1918

Dear friend and Mystifier,

I have just received your letter — dated 9 July — and your poems this very minute. Of course, I'm in prison and am currently in no condition to express anything concrete about your work: will you forgive me for all this?

I'm pleased to live beatifically, like 13 x 18 cameras — It's much like any other way of waiting for the eventual end. I gain strength and save myself for future acts. You'll see what a wonderful helter-skelter our future will be and how it will enable us to kill people!!! . . . I also do some experimenting so as not to get out of practice, right? — but I must just keep my intimate jubilations to myself because of the spies of Cardinal Richelieu . . .

I was right when I said that poor G. Apollinaire wrote towards the end in *La Baïonnette*[156] — yet, he was another who did not "hang himself at the window latch." But, he was already a lieutenant with a broken pate[157], wasn't he? And, he was also decorated — Well.

Perhaps we will bestow upon him the title of precursor — we won't go against ourselves in this.

The sun is full of flies and dubious buzzing mess kits — I need some suits made of good green burlap and also a bartender's white waistcoat — and these women stinking with the dissolvent odour of dirty perfumed underwear . . .

And you, old friend?

J.T.H.

■ 14. II. 18.

Very dear friend,

— In what a depression your letter has found me! — I'm empty of any ideas and a bit resonant, more than usual, no doubt, an unconscious recorder of many things *en bloc* — What crystallisation? . . . I shall leave the war slightly deranged, perhaps like one of those wonderful village idiots (and I even wish it to happen) . . . or else . . . or else . . . what a film part I will play! — With fabulous automobiles, you know the type, with bridges that give way and giant hands that crawl about the screen toward what document! . . . Useless and insignificant! — With dialogues so tragic, delivered in tux and tails behind a palm tree that listens! — And then Charlie[158], leering naturally, his eyeballs calm. The policeman who is forgotten locked up in the trunk!!!

— Telephone, in shirt sleeves among speeded-up people with bizarre jerky movements — William R. G. Eddie, who's sixteen, has billions of black livery slaves, beautiful ashen-white hair and a tortoise-shell monocle. He'll get married.

I will also be a trapper, thief, explorer, hunter, miner, or oil-drillerr — Arizona Bar (*Whisky* — *Gin and Mixed?*), and sweeping exploitable forests and you know those wonderful riding breeches that you wear when using a machine gun, clean-shaven and boasting such good hands at solitaire. All that will come to an end in a fire, I tell you, or, fortune made, in a saloon — *Well.*

— Poor friend, what am I going to do to put up with these final months in uniform? — (they assured me the war was over) — I'm (I can't stand it any longer) at the end of my rope . . . and then THEY are suspicious . . . THEY suspect something — Provided THEY don't disembrain me while I'm still in THEIR power?

— I've read the article on cinema (in *Film*) by L.A.[159] with as much pleasure as I'm able to muster at the moment. There will be some rather amusing things to do once I'm unchained and at liberty.

AND THEN

LOOK OUT!

— Are you going to write to me?

Your good friend.
Harry James.[160]

■ Letter Fifteen
To André Breton

■ 19. 12. 18.

My dear André,

. . . I would also like to see you again — Decidedly, the number of subtleties here is very minute — How I envy the fact you are in Paris and can mystify those who are worth the trouble — Here I am in Brussels, once again in my dear tango atmosphere at around 3:00 a.m. — what a marvellous business it is to sit in front of some monstrous cocktail with a double straw and some bleeding smile — I'm drawing funny pictures using coloured pencils on coarse-grain paper and I mark up the pages for something or other — I hardly know what. You see, I don't know where I am any longer. You spoke to me about some sort of scenic action (you remember — with characters — you specified them) — and then you asked me to do some woodcuts to accompany some poems of yours — Could this be put off for a while? Excuse me for misunderstanding your last sibylline letter. What do you want from me — my dear friend? — 'UMOUR — my dear friend, André . . . this is no trivial matter. There's no question here of any Neo-naturalism — Will you, when you can — explain this for me just a bit further? — I believe I remember that, granted, we decided to leave SOCIETY in a startled semi-ignorance until we can come up with a satisfactory and perhaps scandalous manifestation. At any rate, and quite naturally, I'm depending on you to prepare the ways for this deceptive God, sneering slightly and terrible in any case — You see, how funny it'll be if this true NEW SPIRIT breaks loose!¹⁶¹

— I received your letter in multiple pasted cut-outs that made me very happy — It's very beautiful, but don't you think it lacks some bits of a railway schedule?¹⁶²

. . . Apollinaire did a lot for us and is certainly not dead; besides, he was wise to stop in time — it's already been said, but it's worth repeating: HE MARKS AN ERA. The beautiful things we will be able to accomplish; — NOW!

— I'm enclosing an excerpt from my current notes¹⁶³ — perhaps you can put it alongside the poem of yours, somewhere in what T.F. calls "the gazettes of ill-repute" — What's going on with these last people? — tell me everything. Find out how he has won this war for us!

— Will you be in Paris for a while? — I plan on passing through there in about a month from now and I hope to see you there at all costs.

Your friend.

Harry James.

☐ English army
officers drawn by
Vaché.

■ To signify "experience," the French sometimes use the touching expression *le plomb dans la tête*: lead in the head. We imagine that this results in a certain shifting of man's centre of gravity. We even agree to perceive this as the condition of human equilibrium, an entirely relative one since, at least theoretically, the functional assimilation that characterises living beings comes to an end when favourable conditions cease; and they always cease. I am twenty-seven years old and I don't expect to encounter that equilibrium for a long time. I have always forbidden myself to think about the future: if I happened to make plans, it was merely a concession to certain persons and only I knew what reservations I made within myself. I am still very far from insouciance and I do not admit to finding repose only within the feeling of the vanity of all things. Absolutely incapable of taking part in my own destiny, struck in my highest consciousness by the denial of justice which for me is not excused in the least by original sin, I take care not to adapt my existence to the ridiculous conditions of all existence *here below*. In this, I feel completely in communion with men such as Benjamin Constant (until his return from Italy) or Tolstoy, who said: "If only a man has learned to think, it little matters of what he thinks, inevitably he always thinks of his own death. All philosophers have been thus. And what truth can there be, if death exists?"

I want to sacrifice nothing to happiness: I am not pragmatic. Looking for comfort in belief seems vulgar to me. It is unworthy to suppose there is a cure for moral sufferings. I find suicide legitimate in

■ **Witness:**
Disdainful
Confession
by André Breton

□ André Breton (1896-1966) at the time he knew Vaché. Breton became one of the main players in Paris Dada and then the principal formulator of Surrealist ideas.

only one instance: there is no other challenge to throw at the world but *desire*; not facing a greater challenge than death, I may come to desire death. It is not a question of stupefying myself, which would fill me with remorse. I have given in to it once or twice: it does not agree with me.

Desire . . . the person who said to me: "Breton: confident that he will never finish with his heart, his doorknob," is certainly not mistaken. People hold my enthusiasms against me and it is true that I pass easily from the most keen interest to indifference, which my entourage appreciates diversely. In literature, I have successively been taken with Rimbaud, Jarry, Apollinaire, Nouveau, Lautréamont, but it is to Jacques Vaché that I am most indebted. The time I spent with him at Nantes in 1916 seems almost enchanted to me. I will never lose sight of him, and even though I will continue to make new friendships during the course of future meetings, I know that I will never belong to anyone else with this abandon. Perhaps without him I would have been a poet; he frustrated this plot of obscure forces in me that lead one to believe in something as absurd as a vocation. I congratulate myself, in my turn, at not being a stranger to the fact that today several young writers do not recognize the least literary ambition within themselves. We publish to search for men, and nothing further. From one day to the next I am more and more curious to discover men.

My curiosity, which passionately exerts itself on human beings, is furthermore sufficiently difficult to arouse. I have no great regard for erudition or even, despite whatever ridicule this admission may expose me to, for culture. I received an average education, and that almost useless. I preserved from it, at best, a rather sure sense of certain things (it has been claimed that I have above all a feeling for the French language, this does not fail to irritate me). In short, I know sufficient for my particular need of human knowledge.

I am not far from believing, with Barrès, that "the great matter, for the preceding generations, was the passage from the absolute to the relative," and that "the question is now to go from doubt to negation without losing all moral value." The moral question preoccupies me. The natural fault-finding spirit that I apply to other things would incline me to make the psychological result dependent if, at intervals, I did not judge it above the dispute. For me, it has this prestige that holds reason in check. Besides, it allows for the greatest flights of thought. I love all moralists, particularly Vauvenargues and de Sade. Morals are the great reconcilers. To attack morals is still to render homage to them. It is in them that I have always found my main subjects of exaltation.

On the other hand, I perceive only the very guilty exercise of a weakness in what we call logic. Without any affectation, I can state that the least of my concerns is being consistent. From Einstein, we learn that "one event may be the cause of another only if both take place at the same point in space." This, boorishly, is what I have always thought. I deny as long as I touch earth, I love at a certain altitude, what will I do higher? Still in any one of these states, I never pass the same point again and say: I touch earth, at a certain altitude, higher, I am not the dupe of my images.

I make absolutely no profession of intelligence. It is in some instinctive way that I debate within myself this or that reason, or all other vicious circles. (Pierre is not necessarily mortal. Under the apparent deduction that permits the establishment of the opposite, a very mediocre hoax betrays itself. It is quite evident that the first proposition, *All men are mortal*, pertains to the order of sophisms.) But nothing is more foreign to me than the care taken by certain men to save those who can be saved. In this regard, youth is a marvellous talisman. I allow myself to refer my contradictors, if any are to be found, to the lugubrious warning in the opening pages of *Adolphe* [164]: "I found that no goal was worth the effort. It is sufficiently singular that this impression weakened precisely in proportion as the years accumulated about me. Could it not be that there is something doubtful in hope, and that, when it retires from man's career, this life takes a more severe and more positive character?"

I always swore to myself never to let anything die within me, as long as I could do something about it.

Nevertheless, I observe nature's skill when it searches to obtain from me all sorts of withdrawals. Under the mask of boredom, of doubt or of necessity, it tries to extract an act of renunciation from me in exchange for which there is no favour it does not offer. Before, I never used to leave my place without taking a definitive farewell of all accumulated and intertwined memories, of all that I felt ready to perpetuate in myself. The street, which I thought capable of surrendering its surprising detours to my life, the street with its anxieties and its regards, was my veritable element: like nowhere else, I caught the wind of the inevitable there.

Every night at the hotel where I lived, I left the door of my room wide open hoping to wake up at last with a companion beside me whom I would not have chosen. It was only later, I feared, that each in its turn, the street and this unknown woman, could transfix me. But that is another story. To tell the truth, I am not sure this struggle can be carried off, that of all the instants of which the most customary result is to freeze what is most spontaneous and most precious in the world: on many perspicacious occasions, Apollinaire was ready some months before dying to make all the sacrifices; Valéry, who nobly bore his silence, today authorises the worst deception of his thoughts and work. Not a week goes by but that we learn that some esteemed spirit has "settled down." It seems there is a more-or-less honourable way to behave and that is all. I am not yet worried about knowing what group I am in or how long I will hold on. Until further orders, I approve of everything that can delay a classification of beings or ideas, in a word, maintain ambiguity. For a long time, my greatest desire was to make Lautréamont's admirable phrase mine: "From the unpronounceable day of my birth, I swore an unreconcilable hatred toward the somniferous bed-boards.[165]"

Why do you write? *Littérature* one day asked several supposed notables of the literary world. And the most satisfying answer that *Littérature* extracted after some time is from Lieutenant Glahn's notebook in *Pan*[166]: "I write," said Glahn, "to shorten time." This is the only thing to which I can still subscribe, with the reservation that I believe I also write to lengthen time. In any case, I intend to do so and I call to witness the answer I gave one day when developing Pascal's thought: "Those who judge a work based on rules are, in respect to others, like those who have a watch in respect to those who don't." I continued: "Consulting his watch, one person says: We have been here for two hours. Another says, consulting his watch: It has been only three-quarters of an hour. I have no watch. I say to one: You are bored; and to the other: Time does not weigh heavy on you; because for me it has been an hour and a half; and I do not care about those who say that time weighs heavily on them and that I judge by my watch; they do not know that I judge this by fantasy."

Me, a person who has never let a line pass under my pen which will not acquire some future meaning in my eyes, I take posterity to be *nothing*. Without a doubt, a growing disaffection moreover threatens men after their death. There are already some spirits in our days who do not know whom to follow. We no longer attend to our own legend! . . . A great number of lives refrain from moral conclusion. When we will stop giving Rimbaud's or Ducasse's thought as a problem (to I don't know what puerile end), when we will think about collecting the "teachings" of the 1914 war, it is permitted to suppose all the same we would acknowledge the uselessness of writing history. We perceive more and more that all reconstitutions are impossible. On the other hand, it is completely understood that no truth deserves to remain exemplary. I am not among those who say "In my day," but I affirm simply that a spirit, whatever it be, cannot but lead its neighbours astray. And I do not ask for a better fate than the one I assign to all others.

It is in this manner that the *dictatorship of the spirit*[167], which was one of Dada's passwords, must be understood. From this, one conceives that art interests me very relatively. But today a prejudice gains credit, one that tends to grant to the "human" criterion what is denied more and more to the criterion of "the beautiful." Meanwhile, there are no degrees of humanity, or else the work of Germain Nouveau would be inferior to that of a singer from Montmartre, and naturally: Down with melodrama in which Margot . . . To escape, as far as possible, this human type of which we reveal everything, everything that seems to me to deserve any effort. For me to avoid the psychological rule, even in the least way, is equivalent to inventing new ways of feeling. After all the deceptions it has already inflicted on me, I still hold poetry to be the terrain where the terrible difficulties between conscience and confidence have the best chance of being resolved within the same individual. This is why, on occasion, I show it such severity, why I allow it no abdications. Poetry has no role to play except beyond philosophy and, in consequence, it fails in its mission each time it falls under the blow of any decree of the latter's whatsoever. It is a common belief that the *meaning* of what we write, my friends and I, has ceased to preoccupy us, while on the contrary we deem that the moral dissertations of a Racine are absolutely undeserving of the admirable expression they assume. We attempt perhaps to restore *essence* to the form and for this, it is natural that we should try first to go beyond practical utility. We have hardly anything behind us in poetry but occasional pieces. And besides, is not the proper meaning of a work, not that which we believe is given to it, but that which it is susceptible of assuming in regard to what surrounds it?

To those who, having faith in the theories in vogue, would be eager to determine later which affective trauma changed me into the person who uses this language, I can do no less, before concluding, than to dedicate the following portrait, which will be incorporated into the slim volume of Jacques Vache's *War Letters*, published in 1919 by Éditions du Sans Pareil. Some facts, which this portrait will help to reconstruct, will illustrate in an impressive fashion, I am sure, what little I have said. It is still difficult to know exactly what Jacques Vaché meant by 'umour (without an *h*) or even to know where we now stand in his struggle between the faculty for affectation and for cultivating certain supercilious attitudes. Later, there will be time to confront 'umour in this poetical sense, without poems of course; at least poetry such as we know it. But, I will restrict myself at this time to unravelling a few clear memories.

I made the acquaintance of Jacques Vaché in Nantes, where I was stationed as a temporary intern at the neurological centre until the beginning of 1916. He was being treated at the Rue du Bocage Hospital for a wound in the calf. A year older than I, he was a very elegant, red-haired young man who had studied under Luc-Olivier Merson at the École des Beaux-Arts. While confined to his bed, he used to entertain himself by painting and drawing a series of postcards for which he devised strange captions. Poses, such as you find in men's fashion magazines, were almost the only style he used in these drawings. He loved those glabrous faces, those hierarchical attitudes which you notice in bars. Every morning he spent a good hour arranging one or two photographs, a few mugs and a couple of vases of violets on a small lace-covered table within arm's reach. At that time, I was writing poetry in the style of Mallarmé. I was also going through one of the most difficult periods of my life; I was beginning to understand that I was not going to do what I wanted. The war went on. Echoing throughout Auxiliary Hospital 103a were the shouts of the practising doctor, a charming man besides: "Indigestion? I've never heard of it. There are two stomach problems here: the first, for sure, cancer; the other, more doubtful, an ulcer. Give him two portions of meat and a salad. Don't worry, it'll pass. I'll fill you up yet, old man, etc." Jacques Vaché smiled. We discussed Rimbaud (who he'd always hated), Apollinaire (who he'd barely heard of), Jarry (who he admired), and Cubism (which he distrusted). I think he reproached me for my leanings toward modernism, which have since . . . well, let's not get ahead of ourselves. He reacted to things without snobbery. "Dada" hadn't yet come into existence and Vaché never knew about it during his lifetime. Consequently, he was the first to insist on the importance of gestures and actions, so dear to André Gide. The condition of being a soldier goes well with regard to personal growth. People who have never been put under guard do not know what this means and at certain times feel the need to shuffle their heels. Vaché was a past master in the art of "attaching very little importance to everything." He understood that sentimentality was no longer in fashion and that maintaining his personal dignity demanded not being touched. The primordial importance of this had not yet been underlined by Charlie Chaplin. "We need our art a bit dry," he wrote in one of his letters. In 1916, we hardly had the time to make friendships. The very words *home front* meant nothing. It was everything just to stay alive, and the sole act of polishing rings in the trench or even looking around were seen by our eyes as corruption. Writing or even thinking were no longer sufficient in themselves. It was necessary at all costs to give ourselves the feeling of movement, of noise. Barely out of the hospital, Vaché got a job as a longshoreman unloading coal from La Loire. He spent the afternoon at the port working in the coal-bins and in the evening he would go from café to café, cinema to cinema, spending much more time involved in these activities than is reasonable. He created an atmosphere for himself that was both dramatic and full of spirit while arming himself with a pack of lies that he would toss out with no compunction. (He introduced me to everyone as André Salmon, who was just becoming known as a writer, something that would not happen to me until much later.) At this point, I should say that he did not share my enthusiasms and for a long time he would refer to me simply as "the *pohete*," someone who had not sufficiently learned the lesson of the times. He sometimes strolled the Nantes streets dressed in different uniforms: as a Hussar lieutenant, an aviator or as a doctor. If he happened to walk by, he would ignore you completely and continue on his way without so much as a backward glance. But then, Vaché never offered to shake hands either in greeting or farewell. He shared a nice room on the Place du Beffroi with a young woman who I never really got to know, except for her first name, Louise. Whenever I came by to visit, he had her sit still in a corner for hours without making a sound. At 5:00 p.m. she would serve tea and he would thank her by kissing her lightly on the hand. If what he said is true, they never had a sexual relationship and he was content with merely sleeping beside her in the same bed. Besides, he assured me he had always lived like this. In spite of everything, he didn't love her the less and he always referred to her as his mistress, no doubt foreseeing the question Gide would ask one day: "Was Jacques Vaché a virgin?"

I only saw my friend about five or six more times after May 1916. He left once again for the front, where he seldom wrote to me. (He wrote to no one except, out of self-interest, to his mother about every two or three months.) At around 2:00 or 3:00 a.m. on 23 June 1917, when I returned to the Hospital de la Pitié (where I was receiving treatment), I received a note from him, accompanied by a drawing that I published in his *Letters*. He was in Paris, he said, and in the note he set up a meeting with me for the following evening to attend the première of Guillaume Apollinaire's play *Les Mamelles de Tirésias*. I was to meet him at the Maubel Conservatory, where the play was to be performed. At the theatre, the first act had just ended when an English officer suddenly appeared in the orchestra making a loud commotion: immediately, I realized that this could only be him. He was excited by the scandal provoked by the production. Carrying a loaded revolver, he had come into the theatre threatening to shoot into the audience. To be honest, he didn't like Apollinaire's "surrealist drama." He had judged the play to be too literary and condemned this costumed farce.[168] When we left the theatre, he confessed to me that he was not

in Paris alone. The day before, after leaving the hospital (where he had
hoped to find me), he decided to go out for a walk. Somewhere in the
vicinity of the Gare de Lyon, he had been "lucky" enough to help a
"young woman," who was being brutalized by two men. Since she was
only about sixteen or seventeen, he took this child under his wing.
What was she doing out alone in the middle of the night in the
vicinity of a railway station? That didn't bother Jacques. Since she
complained about being very tired, he offered to take her on the train
in the direction of her choice; and so that is how they ended up at
Fontenay-aux-Roses. Once there, they started walking again and it was
only through Jeanne's continued entreaties that he finally began to
look for a place to stay. This was about 4:00 a.m. A street lamp
extinguisher, who by poetic coincidence was an undertaker's assistant
by day, offered them hospitality. The next day, the day of our meeting,
he got up late and barely had time to reach Montmartre. There,
Jacques asked the girl to wait for him at a grocery store, leaving her
with a few pennies' worth of sweets. At the end of the afternoon, he
left me to go and find her. She was a very young girl of extremely naïve
appearance. He had slipped his military identification card and bag
over her shoulder and she accompanied us to Rat-Mort, where Vaché
showed me some war sketches he had made, notably several studies for
a Lafcadio. Jeanne had affected him visibly and he promised to take
her with him to Biarritz. But, in the meantime, he was going to live
with her at a hotel around the Bastille. There is no need to add he left
the next day alone without looking back any more than usual,
perfectly unconcerned with the sacrifice Jeanne said she had made him
of her life . . . and after two days with him in the studio. I have reason
to believe that in exchange, she gave him a dose of syphilis.

Three months later, Jacques was again in Paris. He dropped by to see me but left again very quickly to go out walking alone in the morning air along the Canal de l'Ourcq. I can still see the long travelling coat thrown over his shoulder and hear the sombre tone he used when he mentioned *a success in a grocery business.*[169] "You'll think I'm missing, even dead, until one day — after all, anything is possible (he used a sing-song voice when pronouncing these sorts of phrases) — you will hear that a certain Jacques Vaché lives withdrawn somewhere in Normandy. He is involved with animal husbandry. He will introduce you to his wife, a very innocent child-type, rather pretty really, who will never for one minute have suspected the peril she has run. Upstairs, only a few books — very rare, let's say — carefully guarded under lock and key, will attest that something indeed has happened." Even this illusion had to be abandoned a short time later. His letter of 9 May 1918, is proof of that. But, the last stage of Vaché's life is marked by that famous letter of 14 November, which all my friends know by heart: "...I shall leave the war slightly deranged, perhaps like one of those wonderful village idiots (and I even wish it to happen) . . . or else . . . or else . . . what a film part I will play! — With fabulous automobiles, you know the type, with bridges that give way and giant hands that crawl about the screen toward what document! Useless and insignificant! — With dialogues so tragic, delivered in tux and tails" etc. The next delirium is more poignant for us than those of Rimbaud in *A Season in Hell*: "I will also be a trapper, thief, explorer, hunter, miner, or oil-driller: Arizona Bar (*Whisky — Gin and Mixed?*), and sweeping exploitable forests and you know those wonderful riding breeches that you wear when using a machine gun, clean-shaven and boasting such good hands at solitaire. All that will come to an end in a fire, I tell you, or, fortune made in a saloon — *Well.*" Jacques Vaché committed suicide in Nantes sometime after

Armistice. His death was admirable in that it could pass for accidental.[170] I think he had smoked 40 grams of opium, although it is believed that he was not an altogether inexperienced smoker. There is also a strong possibility his unfortunate companions were ignorant of his drug usage and while dying, he was able to commit one last *humorous deception* at their expense.

Although I am not in the habit of saluting the dead, retracing this existence here has both pleased and displeased me. You should also know that almost everything I felt then still binds me to this barely discernible life filled with minute problems. I became involved in all the literary and artistic ventures only later and they still hold me only in as much as I appraise them in human terms compared to this infinite measure. That is why everything that can be achieved within the confines of the intellectual domain will always seem to me as mere testaments of the worst servility or complete bad faith. Of course, I love only unaccomplished things and I propose nothing more than to embrace too much. The embrace and domination are the only attractions. And for the moment, it is enough for me to know that one so pleasing a shadow had once danced to the edge of this window from which I am only now beginning to throw myself each day, again and again.   (1923)

■ **Arthur Cravan:**
notes to pp. 14 -
88

■ 1. The most recently discovered case of a possible Cravan double involves an obscure painter named Edouard Archinard. Archinard's work was exhibited at the Bernheim Jeune Gallery in Paris in 1914, and again in 1917, but he didn't attend the openings and no one seems to have known him. He remains surprisingly out of focus in Emmanuel Bénézit's usually precise *Dictionnaire des peintres* (1911-1923): "a painter born at the end of the 19th century, killed during the war of 1914-1918, very few biographical details known." Archinard's name is not mentioned again until 1992, when four of his paintings surface in Paris just prior to the Arthur Cravan exhibition at Galerie 1900/2000. Their provenance is traced to the estate of Félix Fénéon, Archinard's curator and Cravan's friend. The coincidences are too striking to ignore, especially when one observes that Edouard Archinard was one of the pseudonyms employed by Cravan in the pages of *Maintenant*. I make the case for Archinard as a Cravan fabrication and for Cravan as a secret painter in *The Secret Names of Arthur Cravan*, (*Poète et Boxeur*, Terrain Vague, Paris, 1992).

2. Arthur Cravan, *Oeuvres: Poèmes, Articles, Lettres* (Paris, Editions Gérard Lebovici, 1987). The French original of this and all other quotations from Arthur Cravan included in my text can be found in this work.

3. One theory connects A. Cravan to B. Traven. B. Traven was one of the most elusive authors of the twentieth century, whose intense preoccupation with the mysteries of personal identity and nationality was revealed in novels set in Mexico which began to appear a few years after Cravan disappeared there. Traven's talent for creating fictions around his origins exceeded even Cravan's. Another spurious theory suggests a connection between Arthur Cravan and Felix-Paul Greve, a German poet and novelist who was a friend of André Gide and one of the first German translators of Oscar Wilde. Greve's suicide was reported in 1909. As if his association with Gide and Wilde was not enough, it was later discovered that Greve's widow, Else Hildegard Ploetz, was none other than the Baroness Elsa von Freytag-Loringhoven, who knew Arthur Cravan in New York and whose antics in Greenwich Village were often compared to Cravan's in Paris. Loringhoven has been referred to as the "mother of Dada." But I mention this more because years of research, starting with a very cold trail, eventually enabled Douglas Spettigue to prove that Greve's suicide was faked

and that he re-emerged in Canada with a new identity and name. As Frederick Philip Grove he became one of Canada's most distinguished novelists without anyone realising who else he was. See Douglas Spettigue, *FPG: The European Years*, (Oberon Press, Ottawa, 1973); and *Baroness Elsa*, ed. Paul Hjartarson and Douglas Spettigue (Oberon Press, Ottawa, 1992). Such precedents make it difficult to give up the present search.

4. See Dudley Edwards, *The Wilde Goose Chase*, in *The American Book Collector*, January 1957. Edwards offers the first and most detailed account of the Dorian Hope episode to date, providing valuable information he obtained from the principals involved in the case, most of whom are no longer living. The essay is strong on Wilde, but relies too heavily on anecdotal impressions of Cravan.

5. Arthur Cravan was born Fabian Avenarius Lloyd on 22 May 1887 in Lausanne, Switzerland. His father was Otho Lloyd, brother of Oscar Wilde's wife, Constance. Arthur Cravan is therefore Oscar Wilde's nephew. Otho Lloyd changed his surname and that of Wilde's sons (Cravan's cousins, Vyvyan and Cyril) to Holland in order to distance his family from any further association with Wilde after Wilde's disgrace.

6. Edwards. *The Wilde Goose Chase.*

7. Herbert Boyce Satcher, *The "Dorian Hope" Story*, unpublished holograph manuscript, and related correspondence. Clark Memorial Library, Los Angeles.

8. Cravan was a confessed admirer of Poe and Whitman. "After Poe, Whitman and Emerson, he is the most glorious American," he once told a reporter in response to a question about the black heavyweight boxer, Jack Johnson. (Quoted in the *Introduction* to Mina Loy, *The Last Lunar Baedeker*, ed. Roger L. Conover, Jargon Society, Highlands, 1982).

9. Satcher, *The "Dorian Hope" Story*. Satcher's extensive notes on his encounter with Dorian Hope were written thirty years after the meeting took place ("as far as I can remember, I saw him only once"). He relies on Hope's letters, not his own memory, to suggest Hope's homosexuality, quoting, for example, Hope's epistolary promise to "fulfil all requirements asked of me" and to appear at Satcher's place "Madonna-like in a hat of crushed strawberry effect, the shawl left through Hetty Green's will, and the late Lydia Pinkham's pink tights." Was the impersonator using his own voice or ventriloquising to appeal to his clerical benefactor's presumed taste? Cravan favoured boxing tights.

10. Henry Lethbridge, *The Quest for Cravan* in *Antiquarian Book Monthly Review*, (September 1981). Mr. Lethbridge was the first to discover Satcher's brief memoir, and reviews the facts of the Dorian Hope case as reported by George Sims in an earlier issue of the same magazine with a more discerning eye.

11. The identification of Cravan as the "original" Lafcadio was first established by Jean Cocteau in the Gide commemorative issue of *Nouvelle Revue Français* (November 1951). The identification was later made by Bernard Delvaille in his introduction to the first reprint of *Maintenant* (Eric Losfeld, Paris, 1957). *Les Caves du Vatican* (Gallimard, Paris, 1914) appeared in English translation as *Lafcadio's Adventures* (Knopf, New York, 1925).

12. *No One Found Who Saw Wilde Dead: New York Times Correspondent Investigates Report that He is Alive*, in *The New York Times*, 9 November 1913.

13. *Arthur Cravan is Alive!* in Mina Loy, *The Last Lunar Baedeker*, ed. Roger L. Conover (Jargon Society, Highlands, 1982).

14. It is largely because of the character of Arthur Cravan's relationship with Mina Loy — as revealed in his letters to her and her memoir of him — that I remain sceptical about the Dorian Hope theory, even though I am psychologically drawn to it.

15. Arthur Cravan edited *Maintenant* in Paris from 1912-1914. Six issues were published in limited editions at irregular intervals; today they are among the scarcest little magazines associated with the Dada movement. The entire content of *Maintenant* is reproduced in Cravan, *Oeuvres* (Gerard Lebovici, Paris, 1987) and the complete run has been reprinted twice in Paris (Eric Losfeld, 1957; Editions Jean-Michel Place, 1977). An English translation is in preparation.

16. This translation, originally published in the New York avant-garde magazine *The Soil*, April/July 1917, prefaced with this note: *This translation, which does not do justice to the original, is more of a* raccommodage *than a translation.* —*E.C.* The translation has been tidied up a little for publication here, and Cravan's original, and rather unconventional use of inverted commas and dashes to indicate speech has been restored.

17. Roughly, a "failure."

18. Literally: I was lying on my sheets / Like a lion on the sand / So as to strike a

pose / I let my arm hang down.

19. Oscar Wilde assumed this name on his release from prison, when he immediately travelled to France. It derives from the hero of the Gothic novel *Melmoth the Wanderer* by Charles Robert Maturin, to whom he was distantly related. It seems a strange choice for one seeking anonymity.

20. Wilde's French translator.

21. In English in the original.

22. Presumably a reference to a catchphrase of Bruant's. (He was famous for insulting his guests at his cabaret *Le Mirliton*.)

23. In English in the original.

24. In English in the original.

25. A neologism intended to designate someone who tastes and eats other people ideally. [Author's note]

26. André Breton appended this preface to *Notes* when it first appeared in *VVV*: "Independant of the tremendous general interest that they represent, connoiseurs will savour in these pages the climate of pure genius, genius in its *raw state*. Poets will long return to drink from here as from a spring."

27. An important pre- and post-Dada magazine published and edited by Francis Picabia from various cities between 1917 and 1924.

■ **Arthur Cravan: sources and translators**

■ Sources of the texts are as follows: *To Be or Not To Be... American*, signed Fabian Lloyd, appeared in *L'Echo des Sports*, 10 June 1909, translation by Terry Hale. *Whistle* from *Maintenant*, 1, April 1912, translation by Paul Lenti. *André Gide* from *Maintenant*, 2, July 1913, translation by Terry Hale. *Hie!* from *Maintenant*, 2, July 1913, translation by Paul Lenti. *Oscar Wilde Lives!* from *Maintenant*, 3, October 1913. The present translation first appeared in the short-lived avant-garde review *The Soil*, 4, April 1917, and 5, July 1917. *Poet and Boxer* from *Maintenant*, 5, March 1915, translation by Paul Lenti. *Notes* from *VVV*, 1, July 1942, and 2/3, March 1943, translation by Terry Hale. *Arthur Cravan and American Dada*: Buffet-Picabia's article was first published in *Transition*, No. 27, April-May 1938, translation by Maria Jolas.

■ Jacques Rigaut: notes to pp. 90 - 130

■ 28. In *The Dada Painters and Poets: An Anthology*, edited by Robert Motherwell, 1981, p. 111.

29. Paul Eluard, to whom the story is dedicated, wondered by what "miserable abuse" it fell into such hands. (*Le Surréalisme au service de la révolution*, October 1930.)

30. Cited in Pierre Andreu and Frédéric Grover, *Drieu la Rochelle*, 1979, p. 223.

31. Jacques Porel. Cited by Matin Kay in his edition of Rigauts, *Ecrits* (see below).

32. Rigaut occasionally used this variant spelling.

33. Rigaut appears in several of Blanche's memoirs and he often stressed this aspect of his daily life: "Jacques would not come to any decision, however unimportant, without pulling his dice out of his pocket and shaking them on to the table from a rubber cup in order to invite the fates to present him with an omen." (*Portraits of a Lifetime, 1918-38*, Dent, 1939, 34.)

34. Blanche draws the reader's attention to Drieu La Rochelle's *Plainte contre inconnu* (Gallimard, 1925).

35. In *La Révolution surréaliste*, 12 December 1929

■ Jacques Rigaut: sources and translations

■ The translations in this collection have been based mainly on the comprehensive edition of Jacques Rigaut's writings established by Martin Kay (*Ecrits*, Gallimard, 1970). This work also contains a great wealth of biographical and bibliographical detail which is recommended to the reader who wishes to learn more of Rigaut's life and work. The translations here are a selection from those that first appeared in issue 9, volume II of the Atlas Press series *The Printed Head*. All translations are by Terry Hale.

Sources are as follows: *The General Suicide Agency. Agence Générale du Suicide* was not published until 1959 in the collection of Rigaut's writing of that title brought out by Pauvert. The manuscript was formerly in the private collection of André Breton. *Lord Patchogue* was first published in book form in Jacques Rigaut's *Papiers Posthumes* edited by Raoul de Roussy de Sales in 1934. It was substantially revised on the basis of the original manuscript by Martin Kay for the Gallimard edition. Rigaut thought that on 24 July 1924, in the house of Cecil Stewart, he actually succeeded in penetrating to the other side of the mirror. *A Brilliant Individual*, from *Littérature*, 2nd series, 2, April

1922. *Story of a Poor Young Man* from *Littérature*, 1st series, 18, March 1921. *Jacques Rigaut* from *Littérature*, 1st series, 17, December 1920. This was Rigaut's first contribution to the review founded by Aragon, Breton and Soupault and is perhaps the most often reprinted of his works. Although in the Gallimard edition it has been retitled *"Je serai sérieux . . ."*, the original title has been retained for the present edition. The attempted suicide described in the piece probaby took place around March 1920. The essay by Jacques-Émile Blanche originally appeared in *Les Nouvelles Littéraires* in 1930. the English translation by Samuel Putnam, is from his excellent anthology *The European Caravan* (1931).

■ 36. See particularly the *Cahiers du Collège de Pataphysique* 1, 7, and 8-9 and the *Dossiers du Collège de Pataphysique* 21 and 22-24. The *Collège* makes frequent reference to Torma in its internal publications, however, and the issues listed here merely represent the most substantial collection of articles and previously unpublished material.

37. Ruy Launoir, *Clefs pour la 'Pataphysique* (Seghers, Paris, 1969, p. 42).

38. Michel Corvin has gone so far as to suggest that Max Jacob was the actual author of *La Lampe obscure* (*Julien Torma: Essai d'interprétation...*, Nizet, Paris, 1972, pp. 51-52). Such a suggestion is clearly preposterous — although not as preposterous as some of his other hypotheses — and has not been taken up by other commentators. By 1920, Jacob was no longer by turns the unknown poet-mystic and clown, who had befriended Picasso and Apollinaire shortly after the turn of the century. He was in his mid-forties and had already brought out the work on which his future reputation would to some extent depend: *Le Cornet à dés* [*The Dice Cup*] of 1917, a collection of prose poems of peculiar dream-like intensity whose rhetorical aspects, at least, prefigure Surrealism.

39. Max Jacob, *Correspondance*, ed. François Garnier, Editions de Paris, Paris, 1953, vol. I, pp. 187-188, 189-191 and 194-196.

40. i.e. *La Lampe obscure*.

41. A reference to a poem by Torma.

42. Mention must also be made of a posthumous play, *Le Bétrou*, first published in issue 7 of the *Cahiers du Collège de Pataphysique*. This four act drama begins at Act 3 only to conclude at Act 0. At the end of two of the acts most of the characters are killed

■ **Julien Torma: notes to pp. 131 - 198**

(first poisoned and then blown up) only to be resuscitated at the beginning of the following act. The dialogue shows little determination to follow any logical line of development — which is hardly surprising given that the author apparently jotted down ideas as they occurred to him and then juxtaposed them at random to give the final result. If this seems an unlikely recipe for good theatre — even good anti-theatre or theatre of the absurd — it is perhaps worth noting that *Le Bétrou* recently enjoyed a brief but successful run in a theatre in Paris.

43. The date 1925 is obviously a slip of the pen and should read 1926.

44. Daumal's letters to Torma appeared in René Daumal, *Lettres à ses amis* (Gallimard, Paris, 1958), vol. I, pp. 134-137. The replies were published in issue 8-9 of the *Cahiers du Collège de Pataphysique.*

45. An English translation of Daumal's article, as *Pataphysics and the Revelation of Laughter*, may be found in René Daumal, *The Powers of the Word. Selected Essays and Notes, 1927-1943*, ed. and trans. by Mark Polizzotti (City Lights Books, San Francisco, 1991) pp. 15-22.

46. Germain Nouveau.

47. Heroes of Jarry's *Days and Nights* and *Absolute Love* respectively.

48. Refers to Desnos' break with the Surrealists.

49. The paper contained a copy of a poem entitled *Orient.*

50. Translator's note: Torma's word-play presents the translator with many problems. This version of *Euphorisms* is *almost* a complete translation, however a few sections had to be omitted where the word-play became too complex. In the original text the sub-headings were running heads; all have been retained despite some being untranslatable and their necessitating rather too many footnotes.

51. After spending some time in his youth in a Jesuit seminary, Sébastien Faure (1858-1942) became a tireless propagandist for the anarchist cause, he was among the accused in the famous 1894 "Trial of the Thirty."

52. The French *coup de pied de l'âme* is a word play on *coup de pied de l'âne* (donkey's kick), the phrase was used by Léon-Paul Fargue to signify the poet's ability to ignore the mediocrities of the everyday in order to "plunge into the infinite."

53. In the original *Mon moi-toits*, evoking *moi-toi(s)*: I-thou(s).

54. Speak to me of slugs: an echo of the old and well-loved song *Parlez-moi d'amour*?

55. *Dis-pense* with thinking. Play on words: the French *dispenser* means to excuse somebody from doing something, or (as in English), to do without it (as in English, the *dis-* prefix performs what grammarians call a "privative" function): and the French *penser*, of course, means to think; so *dis-pense* here conveys a double sense of doing away with or getting out of thinking *by* thinking.

56. Two fictional characters: stupid & bourgeois.

57. The original *L'oncle d'Onirique* is a word-play on *l'oncle d'Amérique*, the mythical dream-uncle who intervenes to get one out of a financial scrape.

58. Torma telescopes into a portmanteau-word the Kantian dichotomy of *phenomenon* and *noumenon*.

59. In French *Fromage de tête*, in English "brawn," and American "head-cheese," the old-fashioned delicacy made of the chopped, boiled and jellied flesh of a pig's head.

60. A *fiche policière* is an individual's police record, with mug-shots, previous convictions, measurements, distinguishing features, known associates etc.

61. "Are you biting your tail, serpent?"

62. Q, when spoken, approximates to *cul* = arse[hole].

63. Chance boils down to [the will of] God.

64. Here Torma is really packing the meanings in! The Saint Thomas here is Thomas Aquinas, the great Catholic theologian. A *bête de somme* is a beast of burden (such as an ox or a horse). Whilst still a student, Aquinas had earned the nickname of "the dumb ox," on account of his taciturnity and physical bulk. Aquinas's most famous work is the *Summa Theologica*, in French *Somme théologique*; and, in French, one of the extended meanings of *bête* is a fool, a blockhead — hence the possibility of a reading: "the blockhead (or the ox) of the *Summa.*" Finally, taking *somme* in its (etymologically unrelated) sense of "sleep", *bête de somme*, could be read as "fool of sleep" or "dozy brute."

65. A play on words in the French — *une mystique des tondeurs de chiens:* the primary meaning of the verb *tondre* is to shear or clip, as a sheep or a dog; by extension the verb

is used in the sense of fleecing somebody, taking them to the cleaners. There is also the expression *"J'ai autres chiens à tondre"* — "I've got other fish to fry."

66. As well as its surface meaning, the verb *enguirlander* can mean to bawl out, to reprimand.

67. Achras: a pedantic pedagogue in Alfred Jarry's *Ubu cocu*.

68. The *Belle au bois dormant* is The Sleeping Beauty. Eugène Poubelle, when Préfet de la Seine (1883-96) made the use of household dustbins compulsory in Paris; his name, with a lower-case initial, is the ordinary term for that useful object.

69. The original is clearer, *feux des mots* being a word-play on *jeux des mots*: "word-play"!

70. André Gide's *Les Nourritures terrestres* counselled an attitude of *disponibilité*, that is openness to the impulse of the moment and a readiness to accept whatever comes one's way. *Esther*: a religious drama by Racine.

71. An untranslatable pun here on *fausse* (feigned), *aisance* (facility), and *fosse d'aisances* (cesspool).

72. A list of mainly Catholic, and patriotic, authors.

73. Word-play on *scie* (saw), *reine* (queen), and *sirène* (siren, mermaid); and perhaps also a reference to a phrase from Jarry that Torma quotes elsewhere: *La science avec une grande Scie.* (*Le Surmâle*, in *Oeuvres complètes*, II, 247.)

74. A *fontaine* is, of course, a spring or fountain. La Fontaine was the author of highly moral fables.

75. An allusion to Verlaine's book of essays *Les Poètes maudits*, the "damned" poets. Verlaine's studies of Corbière, Desbordes-Valmore, Mallarmé, Rimbaud (and himself) established their reputations and essentially marked the beginning of the French Symbolist movement in literature.

76. Reference to the proverbial phrase *prendre des vessies pour des lanternes*, "to take bladders for lanterns" — to be easily conned, to believe the moon is made of green cheese.

77. The hermit-crab reference is to the last two sections of Breton & Soupault's *The Magnetic Fields*, the first Surrealist book (published in English by Atlas Press), the monocled jelly-fish may be Tristan Tzara, although Breton also affected a monocle in

the early twenties.

78. Luna Park was a famous Paris funfair.

79. Play on the expression *au petit bonheur*, i.e. haphazardly, any-old-how; here with a clear implication "and certainly for the worse"

80. "Lost time": reference to Proust's *A la recherche du temps perdu*.

81. *Pas d'histoires.* Torma's word-play. The French phrase is the equivalent of "Come off it," or "Don't try it on."

82. Bread: echo of the French colloquial expression *Je ne mange pas de ce pain-là* (literally "I don't eat that sort of bread"), meaning "I won't swallow that." Torma heightens the sentiment: *Je ne coupe pas dans ce pain-là* — he won't even cut into it.

83. Literally: having too much.

84. Caiman: a species of crocodile, but in the slang of the École Normale Supérieure, a member of the academic staff.

85. *Caniveau* = gutter, *veau* = calf, *le veau d'or* = the golden calf

86. The French verb here is *saillir*, to "cover" in the sense of the stallion "covering" the mare.

87. *Raison à louer:* play on *maison à louer* (house to let).

88. The French word *nouille*, like the now rather old-fashioned usage of "noodle" has the sense of a "drip" or a "jerk."

89. The celebrated novelist of the Psychological School.

90. The word *pince* has a host of colloquial meanings: starting with a hand, especially a grasping one (cf. the English verb, to pinch, to steal), it can be used in the context of being arrested (as in the English "pinched"); in an extended sense *le pince* can mean the female genitals, as in the American "snatch." Here, "The man-snatcher" might almost do as a translation. However a *pince monseigneur* is also a burglar's jemmy.

91. *Is fecit cui prodest:* the guilty party is always he whom the crime profits. Legal Latin tag, quoted in the celebrated pink pages of the Petit Larousse dictionary — which adds the rider that the maxim should be used only with circumspection.

92. In French: *A l'article d'amour*; echo of *à l'article de la mort, in articulo mortis*, on the point of death.

93. A play on the French legal expression *vice de forme*, faulty drafting in a document.

94. The name of a brand of cigarettes favoured by Torma's friend the writer Léon-Paul Fargue as well as a famous pre-war brand of condoms.

95. Torma's portmanteau-word, telescoping *braille*, text for fingertip-reading by the blind, and *branlette* — wanking, jerking-off.

96. A thoroughly cryptic phrase rather resistant to translation. However *barre* can mean "bar" in the legal sense of "witness-box," and the verb *clouer*, to nail [down] can be used in the expression *clouer [le bec] à quelqu'un*, "to shut them up."

97. Reference to Jaroslav Hašek's immortal *Good Soldier Švejk*.

98. Echo of *Lapsus calami*, a slip of the pen: a friendly slip-up.

99. Word-play on *(finir) en queue de poisson*, to come to an untimely end, to fizzle out, and *queue de poisson*, sting in the tail.

100. *Pense-bête* = literally, "thought-beast," actually a "reminder," or a "crib," etc.

101. See note 116.

102. Pun on the name of the addressee of the letter (Emmanuel Peillet) which is suppressed in the original.

103. Surname of a friend of the addressee.

104. "*Parler synthèse*" in the context of a letter to Peillet refers to the art of using expressions which are ingeniously contradictory.

105. The preparatory class for the prestigious Ecole Normale Supérieure.

106. Roger Pons, Merlen's main teacher at Lille.

107. Templemars, suburb towards the south of Lille where Philippe Merlen's grandmother lived.

108. His parent's house.

109. This sentence, which is written between the lines of the original manuscript, was

obviously an afterthought.

■ Torma's *Euphorismes* was first published privately at the expense of Jean Montmort in 1926, reprinted by Paul Vermont, 1978. The *Letter* by Philippe Merlen appeared as a small plaquette published by the *Collège* in 1955.

    The translation of the text of *Euphorisms* is by Iain White, that of the letter by Terry Hale.

■ **Julien Torma: sources and translations**

■ 110. Towards the end of his life, Jarry himself was also known for strange affected "Ubuesque" mannerisms, which included walking the streets of Paris dressed in a bicycling costume and carrying a loaded revolver.

■ **Jacques Vaché: notes to pp. 199 - 249**

111. "The Disdainful Confession," *Les Pas perdus*, 1924.

112. Cocteau later quit the war, he confessed, because he was having too much fun.

113. Another of Vaché's appropriations from *Ubu Roi*.

114. *Littérature*, 5, July 1919; 6, August 1919, and 7, September 1919.

115. The fifteen letters, along with 64 letters to other friends and family, have since been collected by Georges Sebbag, and published as *Soixante-dix-neuf Lettres de guerre* (Éditions Jean-Michel Place, Paris, 1989). The same publisher brought out an edition of a further 43 letters to Jeanne Derrien, in 1991.

116. Vaché may have been an interpreter for the British, but his Italian phrase should read: *Nome di Dio!* (Good God!)

117. In Alfred Jarry's novel *Exploits and Opinions of Dr. Faustroll, Pataphysician: A Neo-Scientific Novel*, Dr. Faustroll was accompanied on his journeys through Paris by the bailiff Panmuphle and the baboon Bosse-de-Nage (Bottom-Face), who Jarry describes as "a dog-faced baboon less cyno- than hydrocephalous, and, as a result of this blemish, less intelligent than his fellows." (Book II, Chapter 10) Bosse-de-Nage's entire command of French, in fact his only utterance in the novel, was "Ha ha."

118. Vaché's nickname for Breton's longtime friend Théodore Fraenkel (1896-1964), a military doctor during the war was the "Citizens of Poland." The reference is to *Ubu Roi*, in which Ubu becomes king of Poland which, as Jarry put it,

"is to say, nowhere." When the play was performed, the partitioned Poland did not exist as a country. In the play, the entire Polish Army is portrayed by a single man bearing a sign: "The Polish Army." Fraenkel was of Polish descent.

119. Vaché's signature is short for the pseudonym Jacques Tristan Hylar.

120. *Touffaine*, French slang for opium.

121. Title of the poem by Stéphane Mallarmé, *L'Après-midi d'un faune*.

122. A.S.C. (Army Service Corps), B.E.F. (British Expeditionary Force).

123. Franglais for "don't act."

124. *Sârs* and *mimes* were the nicknames for Vaché's group of friends from his Nantes lycée with whom he produced three literary reviews: *En route, mauvaise troupe* (1913); *Le Canard sauvage* (1913-14), and *Les Sârs ont dit* (1914-15).

125. Tzara, Huelsenbeck and other Dadaists wore monocles to poke fun at bourgeois pretensions.

126. Pun with "post scriptum," here meaning an appended hidden message, rendered even more cryptic by being crossed out.

127. Fraenkel.

128. In *Comme dans un bois*, published in *L'Age du cinéma* No. 4/5 (August - November 1951), André Breton related how he and Vaché used to tour the cinemas of Nantes, entering and leaving them at random without checking the times or names of the films playing. This practice had a jarring effect on them and the resulting movie fragments would give them a disjointed or "hypnotic" experience. "What was important," he said, "was that we came out *charged* for a few days."
   Again, two years later, Breton noted: "When I was *at the cinema age* . . . I never began by consulting the amusement page to know what film seemed likely to be the best. Nor did I inquire about the time when the film began. I agreed particularly well with Jacques Vaché in appreciating nothing so much as dropping in at a movie house when what was playing was playing, at any point in the show. And we would leave at the first sign of boredom — of surfeit — to rush off to another movie house where we behaved in the same way, and so on . . ." —André Breton: *La clé des champs* (1953) pp. 241-246.

129. Vaché's word-play (h + amicable).

130. Marie Laurençin (1885-1956), an artist connected with the French avant-garde movement at the beginning of the century. Jacques-Émile Blanche called her "the milk pitcher of cubism," and she was Apollinaire's mistress from 1907-13.

131. Adjective derived from *Ubu*.

132. Reference to one of Vaché's drawings of army life.

133. From Jarry's *Chanson du décervelage* (Disembraining Song).

134. Avant-garde writer Pierre Reverdy (1889-1960) launched the literary journal *Nord-Sud* (North-South) in March 1917. The review, which included works by Apollinaire, Max Jacob, Breton, Aragon, Soupault and others, was named after the Paris metro line that connected the two artists' quarters, Montparnasse and Montmartre. The former Nord-Sud line, now line four, is also known as the Marie d'Issy-Porte de la Chapelle line.

135. Zosimos of Panopolis: a third century Gnostic and author of one of the most hallucinatory texts of mystical alchemy, *The Treatise of Zosimos the Divine concerning the Art*. None of which explains his appearance here, unless this is a coded reference to Vaché's drug-taking.

136. General Gérald Pau was head of the Army of Alsace, formed in August 1914.

137. Poet Pierre Albert-Birot (1876-1967) launched the literary journal *SIC* in January 1916 as a showcase for experimental writing. The title, of course, refers to the Latin categorical affirmative, but also stood for: Sounds, Ideas, Colours. The slim journal ran to 54 numbers before its dissolution in January 1919. The *Practitioner's Journal* that Vaché refers to is the May 1917 issue of *SIC* in which Fraenkel submitted a hoax poem entitled *Restaurant de Nuit*, under the name of Jean Cocteau. The poem was an acrostic with the first initials of each line spelling "PAUVRES BIROTS" (poor Birots), referring to Birot and his artistic-minded contributors.

138. "Pshit" (*merdre*) approximates Jarry's spelling of *merde* (shit).

139. *Les Caves du Vatican*, 1914 novel by André Gide (1869-1951).

140. *Le Poète assassiné* (*The Poet Assassinated*), an experimental novel by Guillaume Apollinaire, was first published in 1916 by the Bibliothèque des Curieux.

141. In *Ubu Roi*, Ubu was the Minister of Phynances.

142. *L'Auberge de l'ange gardien*, by 19th century novelist Comtesse Sophie Segur, popular reading for French children at the turn of the century.

143. Always working on the fringe of the French avant-garde, Jean Cocteau (1889-1963) was the *bête noir* of the Surrealist group and especially disliked by Breton. According to the painter Giorgio de Chirico, the Surrealists would anonymously phone Cocteau's mother in the middle of the night and tell her that her son had been run over by a car.

144. *Les Mamelles de Tirésias*, by Guillaume Apollinaire, was finally performed on 24 June 1917, at the Conservatoire Renée Maubel, directed by the author. Vaché made theatre history through his unique criticism of the play. André Breton described that evening in *Entretiens* (Conversations, 1913-1952), his published interviews with André Parinaud:

The play began about two hours late and, although the work was sufficiently deceptive in itself, the performance was mediocre; and the audience, already annoyed by the late start, caused an uproar during the first act. When the orchestra started playing, another commotion began though I couldn't figure out what caused it: It was Jacques Vaché, who had marched in dressed as an English officer. In order to play the part, he had drawn his revolver and looked as if he were in the mood to use it. I calmed him down the best I could and managed to make him sit through the rest of the production, but not without a great deal of impatience on his part.

Never, as on that particular evening, have I ever again had the opportunity to measure the width of the gap that was going to separate the new generation from that which had preceded it. Exasperated as much by the play's cheap lyric tone and by the cubistic redundancy of the sets and costumes, and in this attitude of challenge before a blasé and sophisticated audience, at that moment Vaché appeared as a seer."

145. Reference to a drawing Vaché included in his letter of 29 April.

146. Vaché uses the term "surrealist," which Apollinaire first used in his programme notes for the 1917 Cocteau-Picasso-Satie-Massine collaboration *Parade*, performed by the Ballets Russes. Apollinaire later subtitled his play *Les Mamelles de Tirésias* "a surrealist drama." However, it was not until 1924 when André Breton issued the first *Manifesto of Surrealism* that the word acquired its current meaning.

147. Unscrambled this reads: "Meet me in La Rotonde for an aperitif." La Rotonde was a popular Montparnasse artists' café.

148. *"Pohète,"* phonetic spelling of "poet," referring to Breton.

149. Breton planned to collaborate with Vaché on a play, which the latter put off. Vaché mentions this again in his final letter to Breton (19 December 1918). In 1920, Breton wrote the play *S'il vous plaît* (If You Please) with Philippe Soupault. It was later published in *Les Champs magnétiques* (The Magnetic Fields), bearing a posthumous dedication to Vaché.

150. A sworn enemy of poetry, the Australian agro-chemist Horace Tograth was responsible for the poet's death in Apollinaire's novel *Le Poète assassiné.*

151. Hero of André Gide's novel *Les Caves du Vatican.* Lafcadio commits the truly "gratuitous act" of murder for no reason.

152. Breton apparently quoted Rimbaud's proclamation "Art is stupidity," from a rough draft of *A Season in Hell,* in a letter to Vaché.

153. Poem by Louis Aragon, published in *Nord-Sud* (March 1918), which he sent to Vaché. *Soifs de l'Ouest* was later published in the collection *Feu de joie* (1920).

154. André Derain (1880-1954), a Fauve, later a realist, painter. The allusion is to a poem about Derain by Breton, later published in *Mont de piété.*

155. When Tristan Tzara was sick, Fraenkel wrote to him on 23 May 1921: "Are you coughing? Spitting? J. Vaché died immediately after I asked him those same questions in writing — but the formula has often failed."

156. Although undated, this letter refers to Apollinaire's death on 9 November 1918. The burial was held two days later on the 11th.: Armistice Day. As the funeral procession was passing by, the crowds ironically shouted: "Down with Guillaume!," referring to Kaiser Wilhelm. The magazine referred to, *La Baïonnette,* published a piece by Apollinaire entitled *Trains de Guerre,* sent to Vaché by his mother.

157. In 1916, Apollinaire had been wounded in the head. Cocteau wrote to the painter Albert Gleizes: "I knew him in his horizon-blue uniform, his head shaved, one temple marked by a scar that was like a starfish. He wore a contrivance of leather and gauze that looked like a turban or a small helmet." (The result of a head wound.)

158. Charlie Chaplin.

159. Louis Aragon's article *Du décor* (On décor) was published in *Le Film,* September

1918. It appeared in English in *The Shadow and Its Shadow*, Polygon, Edinburgh, 1992.

160. One of the pseudonyms employed by Vaché.

161. Reference to Apollinaire's *L'Esprit nouveau et les poètes* (Poets and the New Spirit), in which Apollinaire set forth his ideas on poetry. He originally delivered it as a speech in November 1917 at the Théâtre de Vieux Colombier, it was revised and posthumously published in December 1918.

162. A reference to Blaise Cendrar's 1913 *La Prose du Transsiberien*, with colours by Sonia Delaunay and complete with a rail map. When unfolded, this "simultaneous book" measured over two meters high.

163. Refers to a short text *White Acetylene!*, dated a month earlier, 26 November 1918.

164. By Benjamin Constant.

165. As Alexis Lykiard points out in his translation of Lautréamont's *Maldoror*, the French here is ambiguous, and *planches* can mean also "theatrical boards," i.e. the stage, or "blackboards," i.e. school.

166. Novel by Knut Hamsun.

167. From Tristan Tzara's *Dada Manifesto on Bitter Love and Feeble Love* (1920).

168. Fraenkel's recently published diaries (*Carnets 1916-1918*, Éditions des Cendres, 1990, p. 83) note his disappointment with the play and the appearance at this event of Vaché "of whom we had been so fond at Nantes: ironical, humorous, a fierce hoaxer and liar, scornful and aristocratic." There is no mention of the incident with the revolver however: a surprising omission.

169. See letter of 9 May 1918.

170. Opinion is still divided as to whether Vaché's death was deliberate or accidental.

■ Jacques Vaché: sources and translations

■ The Introduction and translation of *War Letters* first appeared as issue 1, volume III of *The Printed Head* published by Atlas Press. This edition also includes Breton's three other essays on Vaché. The translations are by Paul Lenti.

Vaché's *War Letters* were first published in *Littérature*, 1st series, 5/6 & 7, July and September 1919 and appeared in book form with an introduction by Breton the same year published by *Au Sans Pareil.* Subsequent editions appeared in 1949 (Kra) and 1970 (Losfeld). Jean-Michel Place has since published two further editions augmented with letters to his family and other documentation. *Disdainful Confession* first appeared in *La Vie moderne*, Winter 1923, was based on letters Breton had written to his patron Jacques Doucet between December 1920 and February 1921. It was reprinted in Breton's collection *Les Pas perdus*, 1924.

RELATED TITLES FROM OTHER PUBLISHERS
We are pleased to inform readers of the following publications, all of which carry introductions by Roger Conover (in English):

Arthur Cravan, Poète et Boxeur, a book of critical essays, available from Galerie 1900/2000, 8 rue Bonaparte, Paris 75006.

Mina Loy, *Selected Poems*, to be published by Farrar, Straus & Giroux in 1996, and her novel, *Insel*, available from Black Spring Press, 24 10th st, Santa Rosa, CA 95701.

Mr Conover also invites correspondence regarding the introduction to the present volume, any new information about the various possible pseudonyms of Cravan being especially welcome. He can be contacted via Atlas or MIT Press (Cambridge, Mass.).

RELATED TITLES FROM ATLAS PRESS

ATLAS ARKHIVE I: DADA BERLIN

THE DADA ALMANAC. *Edited by Richard Huelsenbeck, Berlin, 1920. Introduced and annotated by Malcolm Green & Alastair Brotchie. Translated by Malcolm Green, Barbara Wright & Derk Wynand. Illustrations, biographies etc, 176 pp. £12.99 in UK, $19.99 in USA.*

THE DADA ALMANAC was assembled by Richard Huelsenbeck, one of the foremost Dadaists from the birth of Dada to its end, and published in Berlin in 1920 at the high-point of Dadaist activities in the German capital: the Dada Almanac was and is the most important single publication of the international Dada movement. This edition also contains many relevant extra texts and photographs, and biographies of all contributors.

ATLAS ANTI-CLASSICS: FIRST TEXTS OF GERMAN DADA

BLAGO BUNG, BLAGO BUNG, BOSSO FATAKA! *Texts by Hugo Ball, Richard Huelsenbeck and Walter Serner, translated and introduced by Malcolm Green. 176 pp. £8.99 in UK, $15.99 in USA (Uniform with present volume).*

The German contribution to the Dada (DADA MEANS NOTHING! —Tristan Tzara) movement as it unfolded in Zurich during the first World War is still little known. This collection brings together three texts, translated into English for the first time, which were essential for the very inception of the movement.

Included is the *only* Dada novel, *Tenderenda the Fantast,* written by the movement's founder Hugo Ball. It is partially a *roman à clef* recounting the birth of Dada and the author's subsequent love-hate relationship with his monstrous creation, yet it is much more besides. Richard Huelsenbeck's *Fantastic Prayers* was the first Dada poetry collection, and these precocious "Bruitist" poems clearly illustrate how the absurd elements in early Expressionism evolved into the bizarre eloquence of Dada. Finally, Walter Serner's *Last Loosening* manifesto, the first major German manifesto written in Zurich provoked numerous brawls at its various performances and yet is hardly known. In fact it was the scource for many of Tzara's future literary provocations and was deliberately suppressed for this reason.

OTHER ATLAS PRESS PUBLICATIONS

Atlas Press specialises in extremist and avant-garde prose writing from the 1890s to the present day. We are the largest publisher in English of books on Surrealism and have an extensive list relating to Dada, Expressionism, the Oulipo, the College of Pataphysics, the Vienna Group, among others. Many of our titles are only available directly from us, in limited numbered editions (but at normal trade prices).

We also publish various anthologies in related fields, the first two issues of a new series, **ARKHIVE**, are now available: THE DADA ALMANAC, edited by Richard Huelsenbeck is described above. The second issue is THE BOOK OF MASKS, an anthology devoted to French Symbolist writing based on the book of essays by Remy de Gourmont, the third issue will be devoted to Georges Bataille and the Acéphale group, and the fourth to the Fluxus artist/writers Daniel Spoerri, Emmett Williams, Robert Filliou and Dieter Rot. A complete list of all our books is available in our catalogue, available free from:

BCM ATLAS PRESS,
27 OLD GLOUCESTER ST.,
LONDON WC1 3XX.